CURVEBALLS

UNLOCKING YOUR POTENTIAL THROUGH PERSONAL GROWTH AND INSPIRATIONAL MUSIC

Enjoy life
Love Gail

GAIL TAYLOR

Tellwell Talent
www.tellwell.ca

ISBN
978-1-77962-202-0 (Hardcover)
978-1-77962-201-3 (Paperback)
978-1-77962-203-7 (eBook)

TABLE OF CONTENTS

DEDICATION

I dedicate this book to my husband, Harold,
my daughter, Laura, and my son,
Corey, for loving me unconditionally, and
to you, with gratitude, for inviting me to be part
of your path to growth and self-discovery.

FOREWORD

What makes one person able to rise from the ashes like a phoenix while so many of us remain on the ground? You may have dreamed at one time or another of being someone different, of reinventing yourself and living your best life, only to be hit by a curveball or two.

Curveballs—appropriately named—is filled with helpful tools to help you navigate what life throws at you, so you can test your resolve with dignity and continue with renewed vigour on the path you have chosen.

The chances of Gail and I meeting were unlikely, as we live on opposite sides of our country. However, fate has a way of making things happen. We both decided to further our education late in our careers by undertaking MBAs at Queen's School of Business.

My husband Chris and I discovered that Gail was a financial advisor and we were in the market for a great one. She focused on investing in ethical and environmentally conscious companies and that kind of bold thinking aligned perfectly with what we were thinking. Her first questions had little to do with wealth management. "What makes you happy?" she asked. She took our answers and developed a financial portfolio tailored for us. We looked forward to our in-person meetings to experience her bubbly personality, which filled a room with positive energy and giggles. She made finances fun!

Gail recruited me a couple of years later to sit on the board of directors with her for Health Bridge Canada, a nonprofit focused on international health issues for those less fortunate than us. I watched in awe of her ability to extend her energy and influence to contributing greatly to the fundraising goals.

While Gail transformed into a speaker and songwriter, I transformed into a life coach. This was the start of a new path and I have loved every minute of it. Little did I realize that, by taking a completely different direction, Gail and I would cross paths again.

When Gail called me up on a beautiful fall day in October of 2023 to fill me in on all she was working on, I was amazed at how much she could accomplish in a day. My first thought was how lucky I was to have her energy in my life. Gail asked if she could use my coaching services to complement hers as a motivational speaker. I was so honoured she had chosen me.

As Gail focused on writing *Curveballs*, we spoke regularly and soon I was engaged in the editing process. I had no idea of Gail's past and as I discovered the challenges she had faced, I wondered how she manifested her positive energy. How did she manage to fire up her personal nuclear station when all the lights were dim? How could someone turn their life around and never settle for anything less than what they imagine they can be?

While working with Gail on *Curveballs*, I was hit with the big one! In February 2024, through a routine mammogram, a suspicious mass showed up on the image. Fear and tears welled up inside me as I dreaded the thought of telling my ninety-one-year-old mom. She had already lost three of five daughters, two to cancer. The best advice I received was from Gail: to wait until test results were in and the time was right. Keeping calm and positive, I was able to break the news to her in a way that helped her emotional reaction.

My emotional journey continued, as I had lost my sister to breast cancer, and it started to occupy my mind, day and night. I had to do something to lighten up and get perspective. Gail had told me the story of a blob in her eye that looked like a piece of sperm. She named it "Sperm Boy" and used her imagination by giving it a purpose—when she saw it, it was to remind her of her fitness goals! It was just the inspiration I needed. I named my mass "Lumpy," and gave it the purpose of helping me stick with my fitness routine while waiting for my imaging result.

As the cancer testing continued, I found myself researching and thinking about it continuously. Gail mentioned I might try a tool in her book called *compartmentalizing*. She suggested I allow it to occupy my mind for one hour a day. This tactic helped me immensely. When the inevitable thought would invade outside of that hour, I would write it down but knew that the next day I had one hour to think about it. That left me the rest of the day to get back on my path and enjoy my life.

The results showed the cancer was contained, which really made me feel like I had won the cancer lottery. I started to live in gratitude as if I was already cured. Gail encouraged me to use my imagination. I put gems into a small jar with a tight lid and wrote "contained" on it. I was able to use the tools, and especially the music that Gail presents in this book to remain positive; take on only one day at a time because that is all we are given.

You will discover, as I have, that *Curveballs* is no ordinary book. Gail shares her own life's journey with honest, raw truth. She exposes her vulnerabilities, her deepest painful chasms, and the steps she built to climb out and up and up and up! It is structured in an easy-to-read format and will likely serve as a reference long after you have read its last page. Each chapter is titled after a song Gail wrote. The link to the song and lyrics can be found at the end of each chapter. You are truly the beneficiary of her lifelong investment in studying high performance for decades, the results of which she shares freely to help you to learn and apply these inspirational insights to live your best life.

Vicki Schmitt, MBA, PMP,
Certified Professional Coach

INTRODUCTION

When I was twelve years old, my life was forever changed by a devastating event—the untimely death of my father. Losing a parent at such a young age was an overwhelming blow, and I struggled to make sense of the new reality that lay before me. I was so traumatized I initially kept him alive by pretending he was a spy for the government. They needed him to save the world and for everyone's safety they had to pretend he was dead.

My family's financial situation took an unexpected turn after my father's passing. Despite my assumption that we were well off, I discovered over the coming months that the opposite was now the reality. We didn't have the security I had imagined. My father had worked for a mining company that rented homes to their employees. With his passing in March, we were given a strict timeline to find a new place to live. The responsibility fell entirely on the shoulders of my mother, who was in her mid-thirties at the time. In an effort to keep her six children together and to avoid living on welfare, she was able to secure a new home and job in the multifaceted city of Ottawa. This move marked a significant shift in my life, leaving behind a small town in northern Ontario that housed all my friends, and many of my relatives, and adapting to the fast-paced city life where I was a stranger trying to fit in.

As one of six siblings, I felt lost and swallowed up by the vastness of the city. The void left by my father's absence seemed insurmountable, and in my search for comfort and escape, I found myself turning to unhealthy coping mechanisms.

At just twelve years old, I started experimenting with drugs, alcohol, and reckless behaviour. Life continued in a downward spiral for well over a decade. My self-destructive habits led me to a place of messy dysfunction. Hope came when I awoke one morning in my mid-twenties with a simple thought: *There has got to be more to life than this.*

That single thought ignited a fire within me, and I made a conscious decision to change the trajectory of my life. I knew that my future was in my hands, and I had the power to steer it toward a brighter path. With a determination I had never felt before, I embarked on a journey of self-discovery and personal growth.

In the 1970s, during an era of self-improvement and empowerment, I immersed myself in books that opened my mind and soul. I started with Napoleon Hill's *Think and Grow Rich*. It was just the beginning of my newly found appetite for knowledge and wisdom.

Through countless hours of reading, attending seminars, and seeking mentors, I slowly and steadily regained control of my life, or so I thought. Education became my lifeline/passion, as I transformed myself from a high school dropout to a highly educated and ambitious individual.

It was during this transformation that I found my first long-term calling as a financial advisor. I was driven by the desire to become financially independent while helping others achieve their own financial independence, empowering my clients to take control of their finances and secure their futures.

I know firsthand that life can throw curveballs that seem insurmountable, but it's how you respond to them that defines your destiny. I hope that this book serves as an inspiration for you to embrace personal growth, find your strength in the face of challenges, and, ultimately, create a life with purpose and passion.

Here we are, on the brink of a story that's all about self-discovery and chasing dreams. Although I wrote this book for you using my personal stories and the tools that have shaped my journey, it is my hope that you will be able to connect with them and embrace who you are, even when the world pushes you to be someone else. You'll explore how authenticity can change your life, how turning dreams into action can create real impact, and how living a life filled with purpose and passion is more than just a far-fetched idea.

In this book I've combined two writing genres and a bit of music interaction; these are my memoirs in the form of a personal-growth testimonial and guide. My music came later in life and this book is designed around the inspiration that resulted in my writing and composing each song. As a new songwriter, I work with the philosophy that music can transform and positively impact individuals and communities. As discussed in an article in Harvard Health Publishing, Harvard Medical School's online site, music listeners have higher scores of mental well-being, along with less stress and anxiety. Each chapter ends with lyrics and a QR code for accessing the song/video that inspired these stories. This interaction is exciting and I encourage you to listen and watch before going onto the next chapter.

Let's unravel the mystery of being true to yourself in a world that often pulls you in different directions. As you read ahead, my hope is that you'll find something that sparks that fire within you, urging you to step onto your own stage, armed with the tools you need to craft your own best life.

I have always felt deeply honoured, when sharing the narrative of my personal journey, to have received consistent feedback from others who found inspiration in my experiences. Delving into the realms of "personal growth" and "peak performance" starting in the late '70s, I dedicated four decades to crafting what I now fondly refer to as "My Best Life."

I am thrilled to share with you how this life transformation unfolded. My desire is that, through this sharing, you may glean insights to help you create and design the life you genuinely deserve.

It's crucial to note that I haven't pioneered anything revolutionary in this book. Instead, I've diligently applied the wealth of information and tools I accumulated over decades of studying experts in the field. I've used my own experiences to illustrate how my life underwent profound changes and how I managed to cultivate sustainable well-being. Every day, I wake up with a zest for life, a bounce in my step, and a twinkle in my eye. It's this happiness into which I hope you find insight through the pages of this book.

While my personal obstacles may have taken different forms than yours, you'll discover that the challenges we face—what I like to call life's "curveballs"—are universal. We all have a unique story, and it is my sincere privilege to share mine in the hopes of helping you live your very best one.

Throughout my life, challenges have presented themselves in various packages, each contributing to the mosaic of my journey. I am immensely grateful for the opportunity to extend my hand and assist you on your path to embracing your own extraordinary life.

Through the Eyes of Others

The beginning of my journey and the first song is about losing a loved one at such an early age that you don't remember them. I remember my father; however, I have younger siblings that don't, and they inspired this first song, "Through the Eyes of Others." I hope you enjoy the music throughout the book.

THROUGH THE EYES OF OTHERS

BY GAIL TAYLOR AND MALLORY BISHOP

They told me you were tall and handsome
and the pictures would say, they were right
Your laugh they say was awesome
You were so many people's light

I have no memories of who you were
so perhaps the tales are really the lure

I can't understand why you left me
even though it wasn't your choice
It makes me sad because
I don't remember hugs you gave me
I don't even know the sound of your voice
How I wish I could remember one Christmas
or a birthday when you were near
the stories I hear are just covers
told with love through the eyes of others

They told me you were a family man
with a love for kids and fun
It seems so hard to understand
'cause you were gone when I was young

I have no memories of who you were
so perhaps the tales are really the lure

I can't understand why you left me
even though it wasn't your choice
It makes me sad because
I don't remember hugs you gave me
I don't even know the sound of your voice
How I wish I could remember one Christmas
or a birthday when you were near
the stories I hear are just covers
told with love through the eyes of others

Why am I hurting? Why can't I let go?
Decades have passed yet I'm in this dark hole
I crave your approval though it can't exist
My mind's wrapped in pain
from what I cannot miss

I can't understand why you left me
even though it wasn't your choice
It makes me sad because
I don't remember hugs you gave me
I don't even know the sound of your voice
How I wish I could remember one Christmas
or a birthday when you were near
the stories I hear are just covers
told with love through the eyes of others

PART ONE

LIFE ON THE OUTSIDE

CHAPTER ONE

The Game of Life

My Story

Many people spend years—decades, even—in jobs that are safe, but not challenging. Stable, but far from rewarding. I refer to that choice as *settling*. If you are in this situation, you might tell yourself you are staying in this role for your family or for their future. Sometimes you plan to leave these unfulfilling positions as soon as you have saved a certain amount of money, or have paid for your home or schooling.

I have seen firsthand when opportunities present themselves to folks in these situations whereby they pass on the new challenges and the chance to chase their dreams. You may convince yourself to stay where you are because the field you want to join is too competitive, your skills and talents are rusty and insufficient, or you are too old for a new career . . . a refrain many of us have heard, or uttered. I am so thankful I never believed any of these falsehoods.

When I decided to come out of retirement, three years into it, it was to start my own business: Gail Taylor Music. My goal was to become a keynote speaker, using my stories and music to help others become their best selves. When I mentioned this to my new entertainment lawyer, his first reaction was, "Write a book." And so here we are.

If you have read the introduction to this book, you know something about my rather tumultuous early life and how I turned things around. For twenty-five years as a financial advisor, I helped clients with investments and with building retirement plans. I absolutely adored my job and imagined staying in this role until I retired, sometime in my seventies. Things might have worked out that way, but when I was fifty-eight, I started taking piano lessons.

The lessons were meant to be a hobby, a diversion from days spent neck-deep in numbers, analytical thinking, and playing it safe with clients' nest eggs. Instead of just learning an instrument and having a bit of fun, I fell in love with music as it flooded back into my life. After spending two years with my new passion, I decided to retire sooner than planned and dedicate my time to studying this incredible art form. I was financially independent, so I made the decision, at sixty-one, to sell my business and turn over a new leaf.

It was not just an affair I was having with this new interest. I realized I wanted to spend as many hours in the day as possible learning all aspects of music. For someone with no musical background, I was in for an exciting journey and lots of new experiences. Due to advancements in technology, I was able to study online with the Berklee School of Music. It was so exciting. They did not require me to audition. The curriculum was worth every penny of the tuition I paid. I studied bass guitar, piano, keyboard, ear training, and songwriting. After a few years, I began to toy with the idea of reinventing myself as a musician.

When I shared my new passion with people, I was pleasantly surprised by their supportive reactions. "Oh, that is so inspiring," they would say. I heard this often, from people I knew well and strangers sitting next to me on an airplane. It was as if I was suddenly in the same category as mountain climbers and long-distance swimmers. It felt so amazing to know I could inspire others to pursue their dreams.

I began my journey forty years ago, studying personal growth and peak performance, as I mentioned in the introduction. There is no end in sight. I am still a work in progress—as are you: always learning, always growing. To stop searching for my best self would be like stopping bathing or brushing my teeth. This is the lifestyle I have chosen, with my personal development as a constant. Sometimes it runs in the background of my life, when family, friends, and career are my focus; other times, growth is front and centre.

Simply being aware of a situation isn't enough to make a change, but it's the crucial first step. Once you understand what's going on, you can start looking for solutions. In the next section, we'll introduce some practical tools you can use to take action, especially if you're thinking about making a change.

Tools for Thought
Limiting Beliefs Be Gone

If we could look through the ideas swimming around in virtually any person's head, we would likely find a few limiting beliefs. We can all relate to harbouring these self-defeating thoughts; however, you could build awareness around where limiting beliefs show up for you, and remove them from your mind like gardeners remove weeds from their cherished crops.

Before we talk more about defeating the beliefs that hold you back in life, we will define "limiting beliefs." First, the adjective "limiting" is not one you would want to use frequently if you are striving to become your best self. We can focus on perceiving our possibilities and abilities as having few limits. The second word, "beliefs," is also important to consider. We are not talking about facts when we discuss limiting beliefs. They are not necessarily logic or fact-based thoughts, such as two plus two equals four. Beliefs, limited or not, are simply ideas you have based on your past experiences. Unfortunately, they can manifest as a thought or state of mind that you think is the absolute truth and that is what can stop you from doing certain things. They can also be formed by well-meaning people trying to protect you from hurt or embarrassment.

Limiting beliefs are something you might have adopted at an early age, accepting them as facts. You didn't do well on a math test so decided you couldn't work with numbers . . . ever. Nerves got the best of you during a class presentation, so you avoided public speaking for the next three decades. A Grade 3 music teacher told you you couldn't sing, so you never sang again. This is NOT cool, but I actually met a young woman in vocal classes that experienced this, and she had a beautiful voice.

Obviously, beliefs can wield enormous power over your life. The people who have mastered the power of belief are the ones who have learned that self-fulfilling prophecies often manifest in their lives. This explains the optimistic nature of the predictions they make. I fit squarely into the optimist box, and I am constantly and affectionately informed by my husband, Harold, that I wear rose-coloured glasses. Heck, I sleep in them!

I came across this saying early in my journey: "If you think you can, you're right, and if you think you can't, you're right." How can both possibilities be true? Both possibilities consider the incredible influence your beliefs have over the outcomes. Limiting beliefs can have the power to shut down your dreams before you even start to chase them. The upside is that, once you learn to recognize these adverse beliefs, you can challenge them, which results in their losing their ability to interfere with your growth.

I have found over the years that people have limiting beliefs of various types. They tend to contain phrases like, "I cannot," "I will never," "There is no point in trying," and "I tried that before and it didn't work, so no use trying again." They often grow stronger when they are allowed to take up permanent residence in your head. Repeated enough, they become part of you. I have one I'll share. "I grew up in a family that had no desire for material goods, so I must be damaged for wanting a sports car or a luxury coat." You can become so attached to these limiting beliefs that you feel threatened when something or someone challenges them.

Imagine your optimistic friend is encouraging you to go back to school (for my friends, the optimist would be me). "You would be great at operations management," the friend says. "Think of everything you could do with that degree." However, your limiting belief refuses to accept this possibility.

"Why bother?" you respond. "No program would accept me. Do you know how many years it has been since I was in school?"

You have just handed the limiting beliefs another victory, probably without realizing that you are stating a belief, not a fact.

There are multiple programs for most educational paths. Do any of them refuse to accept students over age thirty? Forty? I was fifty-five when I decided to earn an MBA. I was older than some students who pursue this degree, younger than others. Yes, it may have been your experience that most students belong in a given age category. It also may have been your experience that some people do not gain acceptance to their program of choice. But our experiences do not justify giving in to the limiting beliefs. There are always possibilities outside your own limited experiences.

In your quest for fulfillment, you will face hurdles, and you might even tend to focus on the forces outside your control. Remember, you can learn to master your own thoughts and attitudes but not those of others. To make a conscious decision to challenge limited thoughts when they pop into your head is to give yourself an incredible gift and a powerful tool to discover your best self. You can lead the life you dream of leading.

You have your own unique map based on your past and how you've processed your experiences. Think of it as a quilt with all the stitches and swatches and colours and textures. It may contain areas that need attention because they are holding you back. Another person's patterns and colors may look very different from yours, even those of a sibling who shared the same childhood. Remember, we are all wired differently, and have our own perception of all the things we see and hear.

When you imagine your life as you wish it was, how often are the changes you would like to make internal and how often are they external? Where is the balance? You might imagine yourself as more stylish, possibly wearing more expensive clothes and living in beautifully decorated homes. If I ask you why, your answer will be an emotional response: you *feel* it. It will mean you will feel healthier, or it will eliminate feelings of worry you have about money or security.

The key is to imagine yourself thinking and feeling in positive, self-affirming ways. It's about doing the internal work to meet your external goals. It's about concentrating on things that will bring you closer to happiness and fulfillment. Remember, money or status does not confer personal growth or well-being.

Well-being starts within; it is rooted in substance and grows outward, influencing all aspects of our lives. When you attempt to derive feelings of satisfaction from your possessions and bank accounts, you may find the reward temporary and lacking sustainable fulfillment. Having said that, I love driving a sports car, travelling business class, and experiencing a lot of the finer things in life. I worked hard to get them, and I enjoy them very much. I, however, would not define myself as materialistic. Materialism is defined as "a tendency to value material possessions and physical comfort as more important than spiritual values." That couldn't be further from who I am.

I have never thought any object I own is more important than the intangibles in life. Money, and the things it can buy, are simply tools. Just as someone finds a hammer or wrench a useful timesaver and force multiplier, money often allows me to do many things faster and better.

Using money to travel is something I particularly enjoy. Having visited many parts of the world, I am fortunate to have met people from different backgrounds. Most of the people I have encountered have been delightful, a few less so, and I have learned that the size of a person's bank account tells me nothing about that individual's morals and values.

I don't believe that owning a luxurious home makes a person unprincipled, nor do I believe that living a minimalist lifestyle somehow confers ethical superiority. People live according to their values, and, yes, I value the experiences money affords me. For me, there is no conflict in enjoying a professional manicure and also offering material help to people in need, or family. I value both unapologetically.

I share this because I don't think material possessions and status will free you from your limiting beliefs. It takes time and a certain detachment to learn to recognize that some beliefs may stand like roadblocks between you and new vistas. Practising self-care and self-compassion is more likely to loosen the grip of limiting beliefs: if you heard that someone close to you was convinced that trying to learn a new skill was hopeless, wouldn't you remind them of their talents and tenacity? Reminding *yourself* is equally important. It's up to you to free yourself from the limiting beliefs that hold back your progress and to give yourself the mental and emotional space necessary to accomplish what you desire.

Looking at the world with limiting beliefs is like viewing your surroundings through a dirty window. When you clean the window, clearing away limiting beliefs, things look much brighter. Possibilities for your best life stretch to the horizon and beyond. Now you are seeing your life and potential as they truly are. They are impressive! Removing those limiting beliefs gives you an unobstructed view to an exciting future. Remember to question *everything*. Be your own devil's advocate.

Put these beliefs under cross-examination

Question your internal dialogue and learn to identify what your limiting beliefs are. It doesn't even matter what created them. It's about challenging them and moving forward.

Do they stand up to scrutiny? Become a kind of investigative reporter on the stories that affect your life, relentlessly searching for your truth.

Imposter Syndrome

Once you have accomplished something you desire, you will sail through life feeling confident, correct? It happens to some people, but countless others suffer from something we call imposter syndrome, where a high-achieving person sees themselves as a phony.

Joining the world of music so late in life without a doubt had its challenges. Imposter syndrome reared its ugly head with some of my internal dialogue: Can I call myself a musician when I'm in Grade 4 with piano lessons? Can I call myself a musician if I'm not skilled enough to play live? Can I call myself a songwriter when I need help to create the melody? Can I call myself a producer when the recording studio is engaged in activities far beyond my skill level? I decided I could.

The good news is, I wasn't alone. It's important to realize this about imposter syndrome: Billie Eilish, Lady Gaga, and David Bowie all experienced it at certain points in their careers. For me, it was about accepting where I was in the journey and embracing the adventures life threw my way.

I don't try to pretend I am someone I'm not or that my skills are more developed than they are. I know the reality of my situation. Practice is still the name of the game. Self-awareness and emotional maturity can both go a long way in understanding and accepting your current reality. When you can accept the truth about where you are in your journey, you will be closer to freeing yourself from the confines of imposter syndrome and can view your accomplishments realistically and with pride.

Imposter syndrome is not applicable to a person employing the "fake it till you make it" survival strategy. When you are new to a job, or new to any activity in general, there is a period of unease and uncertainty. It is normal to have self-doubt in this situation, but know it will come to an end as you find your footing.

Highly educated and successful people with extensive training in their fields report experiencing imposter syndrome, as you read in my example above.

You might fear that you will somehow be "found out," that others will realize you are not as competent or as knowledgeable as you appear. Like limiting beliefs, imposter syndrome is a habitual thought pattern that gnaws away at your confidence, at your perception of reality, the way termites eat through wood. Like limiting beliefs, when challenged with facts and empathy, the imposter feeling that one goes through will dissipate. And remember: if the brave face you show the world begins to feel false, it is a good time to realize that even the most pedigreed professionals experience this type of anxiety from time to time. Work through it and let it go!

Lifelong Learning

One could argue that, in this day and age, being a lifelong learner has become a requirement. The rate at which information changes in our world is staggering. As people around the globe gain access to the internet, we can share words, images, and data at lightning speed. Technology hurtles us forward, while fields like law and medicine struggle to keep pace.

Professionals in many scientific fields find the information that guided them a few short years ago is out of date. They must spend a good part of their careers staying current on countless developments and trends.

I pride myself on being a lifelong learner. It is never too late to study, explore, and expand your horizons. The benefits you can reap from these activities go far beyond those of "keeping busy." Engaging in studies over the course of your life is good for the brain. It boosts cognition, mood, and creativity. Continuous learning will frequently put you in contact with others, enhancing your interpersonal connections, which is also an added health benefit.

Lifelong learning is for life. Plenty of senior citizens had little use for the internet when it first became available. Why use the computer to order a book when you could go to the library and borrow one or the store and buy one? When they learned they could see photos of their children and grandchildren on the computer, and even video chat with them, computers became a part of their lives, a technology that brought people closer. My ninety-four-year-old mother takes to her iPad each day to check her email, find out how the family is doing on Facebook, perhaps attend a mass service, or google what the weather will be in her area before she steps out for her walk.

Anna Mary Robertson Moses was busy raising her ten children for much of her adult life. When she decided to dedicate herself to painting at the age of seventy-eight, "Grandma Moses," as people called her, was able to develop talents that had lain dormant for decades. She produced over 1,000 paintings, often featuring charming rural scenes. President Harry S. Truman presented her with a Women's National Press Club Award trophy, having admired her talent and productivity.

Twenty years ago, songwriters like me couldn't bring their songs to life singlehandedly. They needed someone else to approve their work and record it. Now, we can hire a recording studio and studio musicians and use an independent artist distributor to send our very own masterpieces to a worldwide audience. You can listen to my music on all the streaming platforms and watch my music videos, complete with captioned lyrics on YouTube alongside all the record label Top 40 artists.

There has never been a better time, as our society dispenses with outdated notions of what interests are appropriate for one's expressed gender, age, or cultural background. With the internet, you can take classes from your couch, rarely if ever setting foot in a classroom.

Fields of study are more varied than they were twenty years ago, even ten. People can now study developments in nutrition, psychology, and technology that few people knew of in the twentieth century. Accepted theories can be debunked and replaced as we learn and question. Like many areas of your life, learning only moves you forward. What subject have you always wanted to study? Now is the time. Lifelong learning is just that: *lifelong*. No need to stop.

Reinvention

If necessity is the mother of invention, our short attention spans are the mother of reinvention! To keep things interesting, for ourselves and others, it is desirable, and even necessary at times, to reinvent ourselves.

Another reason we might give ourselves internal and external makeovers is because we live and work longer than in years past. Many people happily choose to work beyond the traditional retirement age. If they follow a purpose or passion as their career, they often see no reason to stop working. Clint Eastwood and Betty White were still going strong in their nineties and my favourite, Mick Jagger, is touring at eighty!

As mentioned earlier, our society moves at an increasingly fast pace. Industries spring up, become profitable, and collapse over a decade or less. In recent years, the media has drawn our attention to the significant role artificial intelligence is beginning to play in our lives. There are those who fear their jobs (in fields from medicine to fast food) will become the responsibility of machines that can reason better than humans can.

Clearly, modern society is extremely dependent on computers, but we have been here before. People worried that personal computers would replace humans in the financial and business spheres. There were concerns that microwave ovens would mean the end of healthy cooking and eating. These scenarios have not materialized, in part because humans' connections to one another are impossible to replace. Interpersonal relationships, whether they take place in a kindergarten or a construction site, give meaning to the actions we take.

All this is to say that, while the industry you work in may find itself eclipsed by a shiny new thing, you can reinvent yourself. You can bring all the skills and experiences that you have developed because they are transferable. Your communication skills, your ability to connect with people you have just met, your trustworthiness, whatever you bring to the table still exists. You are still valuable and impossible to replace with a bot, no matter how well designed. Be prepared to reinvent yourself at least once in your career and in your life.

In the chapters "Dreamin' Bout the Good Life—Living with Purpose at Work," we talk about how growth is necessary for you to become your best self. Reinvention is simply another facet of this need to experience a range of possibilities. Embrace transformation. Just as baby birds learn to fly, growth is a natural part of life. Your reinvented self is ready to soar.

Consider all possibilities, even the remote ones. You might unintentionally respond to societal pressure, whether obvious or subtle, to conform to traditional and sometimes outdated definitions of success and happiness. You might be in that group of people who realize later in life that they spent a decade or two working diligently to achieve something others convinced them they should want, only to find they were following someone else's dream.

It is understandable that people close to you may want their version of stability and security for you. They may not want to see you struggle with uncertainty, especially with respect to your financial and occupational situations. Yet some of you have passions and cravings that might take you in a different direction and they also *deserve your attention*. They are like breadcrumbs that form a trail to your authentic self.

The freedom to pursue these possibilities is another benefit of living in the twenty-first century. Social mobility is real, and society is fluid. We are not destined to lead lives virtually identical to those of our parents and grandparents.

If you want a new career or have been forced to look for one, deciding what you want as your next chapter can start with passion and purpose. We will delve into this more deeply in the chapter devoted to these two core concepts. However, a start is to make a list of the things you love to do and the things you care about, and work backward using this information. Are there any job possibilities?

Here is a rudimentary example:

You love:

- Animals—cuddling with my dog, going to the dog park
- Hitting the gym
- Swimming
- Singing
- Playing video games
- Playing with children

You get the idea—new career options:

- Become a veterinarian, work at a veterinary clinic or ethical pet store, volunteer at a humane society, start a dog-walking business
- Become a personal trainer, work at a gym or in fitness at a community centre, coach a sports team
- Become a lifeguard, train for swimming competitions
- Become a vocal artist, backup singer, or studio recording artist; join a band
- Learn to code games, become a game inspector—gaming is a wide-open industry; check it out
- Open a daycare, become a kindergarten teacher

Another point about reinvention is the transferable component of everyone's skills.

Here are examples:

<u>Skills for a Sales Representative</u>

- Communications
- Negotiation
- Relationship-building
- Persuasion

Alternative Job: Business Development Manager

In this role, you would still leverage your sales skills, but with a focus on identifying new business opportunities, building strategic partnerships, and expanding market reach.

Administrative Assistant

- Organizational skills
- Time management
- Attention to detail
- Customer service

Alternative Job: Office Manager

As an office manager, you would utilize your organizational and administrative skills to oversee the day-to-day operations of an office or department, including managing schedules, coordinating meetings, and handling administrative tasks.

Project Manager

- Leadership
- Time management
- Problem-solving
- Budget management

Alternative Job: Event Coordinator

As an event coordinator, you would utilize your organizational and coordination skills to plan and execute events, including conferences, trade shows, and corporate events, managing logistics, budgets, and vendor relationships.

Teacher

- Communication skills
- Adaptability

- Classroom management
- Curriculum development

<u>Alternative Job: Corporate Trainer</u>

Transitioning into corporate training involves utilizing your teaching skills to develop and deliver training programs for employees, focusing on skill development, product knowledge, and professional development.

I know I gave quite a few examples in the above section, but I wanted to emphasize that reinventing yourself doesn't necessarily mean starting all over. You have experiences, skills, and knowledge to follow you on your new venture and there is a lot of value in everything that has led you to this point.

The Game of Life

This chapter started with my story of reinventing myself: from a career in finance, to a retired person studying music, to an entrepreneur with a start-up business as a keynote speaker using her music to help others become their best selves. The game of life is what you make it. It is not defined by your past and the sky's the limit.

THE GAME OF LIFE

BY GAIL TAYLOR AND MALLORY BISHOP

Time changed, time changed
it really shifted
One world for another
No, not yet gifted
Was it too late? Too late?
Why had I waited?
I just wanna make the music
not yet created

Starting down a path that might need changin'
Searching for the song I should be playin'
Everybody knows the chance I'm takin'
Everybody plays the game of life

Five years, five years
still don't feel gifted
One day, then another
Some clouds have lifted
Will my time come? Time come?
I'm not deflated
I just wanna make the music
not yet created

Starting down a path that might need changin'
Searching for the song I should be playin'
Everybody knows the chance I'm takin'
Everybody plays the game of life

What's new? What's new?
Will I have drifted?
One future for another
I might be gifted
So I'll play on, play on
Someday I'll make it
I just made a melody
and life was created

Starting down a path that might need changin'
Searching for the song I should be playin'
Everybody knows the chance I'm takin'
Everybody plays the game of life
Everybody plays the game of life
Everybody plays the game of life

CHAPTER TWO

Dreamin' Bout the Good Life

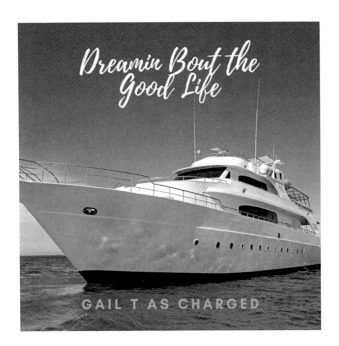

My Story

It was 1979 and I woke up one morning, squinting against the sunlight streaming through the blinds, looked around at the mess I'd made—in both my room and my soul—and thought: *There's got to be more to life than this.*

That small bit of hope sparked a fire within me, and I made the conscious decision to change the trajectory of my life. I knew that my story was my own to write and that I had the power to fill it with brighter pages.

I was a somewhat functional addict and my goal was financial wealth. I wanted "My Good Life" and to be a millionaire. At the time, I was a high school dropout with no connections and no clue how I was going to achieve this. Setting goals and believing in my ability to achieve them was the gamechanger.

The truth is that life isn't always going to deal you a winning hand. Sometimes, you'll find yourself in situations you might not have planned for or even wanted. With the hands I had been dealt I certainly hadn't expected to have such an awakening.

You can't always control what happens to you, but I believe you can learn to control how you handle it.

I know it's a cliché, but a shift to a positive attitude changed my life by giving me the strength to achieve my goals. When I let go of the negativity, life became so much more fulfilling, dynamic, powerful, and fun.

It all came down to managing my thoughts. When I noticed my thoughts veering away from what I was working toward, I'd catch them and shift the internal dialogue. I call it, "Garbage In, Garbage Out," and what that means to me is when I find myself in my head with thoughts that are contrary to what I'm trying to manifest, it becomes critical to catch it and shift the dialogue. It is like taking out the trash!

Here's an example of my approach: as I'm completing a "call for speaker proposal," I might think, *Why would they hire me as their keynote? The audience probably already knows everything I have to say.* If I allow my thoughts to continue along these lines, next thing you know, I'm thinking, *and they're not going to be willing to pay my fee when there are so many other speakers to choose from—some even work for free.* This is where my learned behaviour kicks in and I do not allow my thoughts to continue along these lines. I stop them in their tracks and order them to do an about-face.

SHOUT IT—**GARBAGE IN, GARBAGE OUT**—
THE LOUDER, THE BETTER!

REPHRASE: "I am excited that I found this event." Filling out this proposal and reviewing the event theme—"OMG! I am the perfect fit! I love that I will be able to share my personal journey with these folks and inspire them to become their best selves, to go after their dreams and understand that working through life's challenges is always doable."

Sometimes I'll repeat my new phrase a few times to make sure my subconscious gets the message.

I learned this technique from a famous runner from Toronto, Gayle Olinekova. She wrote a book called *Go for It!* Her book made me feel inspired, capable of doing anything. All I had to do was think it. I also like to use physical objects to remind me of this mindset. I designed a line of pendants with inspirational phrases on them, like "I got this." I use these as tactile items and just rub them. The physical movement goes hand in hand with the mantra: *Garbage In, Garbage Out.*

Whatever you need, whether it is auditory, visual, or tactile, use it to help yourself remember to reframe negative internal dialogue. Try my method and tell yourself a story about how you plan on succeeding in some activity, adventure, work project, etc.

I talk to my subconscious like it is another person and get excited about designing my life. Instead of thinking, *Today is going to be a bad day,* think instead, *Today is going to be great!* Before long, you will *know* you are going to have a great day.

At the end of the day, our life is what it is, but you play a bigger part in this than you might realize. If you believe that your day is going to be terrible, it probably will be, because that's what you've trained your brain to believe.

It's time to retrain your brain to stop sabotaging your dreams and manage your thoughts instead.

Growing up, I didn't really consider the kind of life I wanted. I don't think many of us do. Instead, we take what life gives us. We take the job offered to us, pursue something we know, go into the family business, and stay close to home.

In other words, we let it happen to us. That's not necessarily a bad thing—it's just that when we do that, we tend to get stuck in our comfort zone. We say things like, "Oh, I'll do that one day. . . ." But suddenly, one day becomes one year, becomes two, becomes five, becomes ten, becomes . . . if we're not careful, a lifetime.

Bronnie Ware, an Australian palliative care nurse, spent countless hours by her patients' bedsides, offering solace in their final moments. She says that every patient finds peace before they depart, but they *all* have regrets.

They all wish they'd done *something* differently. Most often, she heard that they regretted working so hard, not having the courage to voice their feelings, not staying in touch with their friends, and not letting themselves be happier.

But amidst the stories they shared with her, one regret echoed louder than others: "I wish I'd had the courage to live a life true to myself, not the life others expected of me."

A lot of us might think that regret is just part of life. After all, studies have found that 90 per cent of adults have deep regrets. As children, we believe that our hopes and dreams will all come true. And they can, but not without a little magic dust, creativity, and design from you.

As mentioned at the beginning of this chapter, I started sketching a new design for my life when I had the realization in my twenties that there must be more to it than drugs, alcohol, and reckless behaviour.

So, I embraced education, and became a lifelong learner and a financial advisor. I went from being a high school dropout to acquiring an MBA from Queen's University, and IMCA's certified investment management analyst (CIMA) designation through the Wharton School of Business. I even completed executive training at Harvard Business School on microfinancing in developing countries.

While I underwent this shift, I never stopped studying personal growth and peak performance. I have been actively involved in this space for forty-five years. I don't just read books. I study them and follow through with the suggestions.

And now: *Wow*, what a wonderful place to be in my life and journey! But I didn't end up here by accident—I created this for myself.

We don't have long on this earth; on average, we'll live to be about eighty or ninety nowadays.

We deserve to spend those years loving our lives and loving what we do.

So, I implore you to set those lofty goals and follow through on them. To live and, more importantly, work on purpose. When you think about it, our work time makes up almost half our waking hours, which means our work lives *are as significant as* our personal lives. *As important as your personal life.* I recommend you choose a job you *want*.

Tools for Thought

Many people tend to think their best lives involve financial security, fulfillment, and maybe some exciting possibilities. The thought is that, once we have earned the amount of money we deem necessary for financial security, we should have fewer worries.

It seems simple enough, but for too many people, living their best lives remains a dream. Not everyone knows how to make it a reality. With or without money.

It is as if living our best lives is a concept, a place people are trying to reach and hoping to stumble on through the events life is throwing at them. That's a little tricky. Alternatively, building a roadmap that establishes where you are and where you hope to go creates unlimited possibilities.

Where are you on your journey? For some people reading this, especially those who want to change careers, it might begin with education. Degrees, licenses, and other credentials are necessary for many of your dream positions. Some of you in this category may have completed the educational requirements and are ready to begin expanding and refining your professional skills.

It's important to remember that your best life is a journey, not just a destination. You can embrace your abilities as the vehicles that will take you there, and your beliefs, your passions, your dreams, as the fuel that keeps you going. This would make the goals the tangible benchmarks you create and reach along the way.

The journey is your life, so sometimes reaching a goal may just be a chapter that will pivot, like attending school or getting training to get to the next level, and the key to happiness is embracing every stage. Knowing that you have the ability to create an achievable goal helps you move forward when the terrain is challenging.

Life throws curveballs at us and puts curves in roads we expected to run smooth and straight. You can prepare for your travels by learning how to act and *react* when life deviates from your plans. I'm sure there are readers amongst you that have had to take a time out from your plans to help an elderly parent through their final years or to take care of a child with special needs. Maybe you needed to heal yourself from a major surgery or an unsustainable business venture. The point I'm making here is that life doesn't always go according to plan—and that's OK. We adjust, rework our expectations, and use the situation as a life lesson, doing our best with what we have.

Now let's get back to creating that best life. . . . Once you've sketched the roadmap, it is time for action. I truly believe that follow-through is the only real difference between those that succeed and those that don't. Intention is just that. Intention. You need follow through to make that intention a reality.

There are several factors that will play into this, including scheduling your time accordingly. Consult the calendar. I've dedicated a whole chapter to time management, sharing how I was able to get a handle on priorities. Without a doubt, this was a major gamechanger for me.

You can now move beyond dreaming about the good life and start planning what the journey looks like. Your best life can start today. Sure, working through past patterns that you need to break and building new strengths like positive internal dialogue will take some time—but that's OK. You set your sights on your happiness and start today, the first day of the rest of your life.

Self-Confidence

Abstract and intangible as they are, goals and confidence play a significant part in our lives. Life is forward motion, a mountain to climb, and a dream to realize. Self-confidence is a kind of accelerant, powering us out the door to achieve our goals. Not easily defined or measured, our belief in ourselves is, perhaps surprisingly, one of the most important qualities needed to send life's curveballs flying.

It is useful to develop a clear understanding of what belief in ourselves looks like. While a person plagued by imposter syndrome (discussed in the chapter "The Game of Life") suffers from a lack of belief in themselves, a self-confident person feels entitled to success, accolades, and financial rewards for their hard work. Simply put, when we have a deep-rooted belief in our ability to follow the path we have designed for ourselves, we are sure to find success.

Dream Boards

Speaking of bigger pictures, dream boards are an excellent way to remind us to stay focused on engaging in meaningful actions every day. While we talked about creating roadmaps of our path to success earlier in this chapter, we can think of dream boards as guides in their own way, giving us a daily visual of the life we are living and creating. They show us highlights of what is important to us. I've been creating dream boards for decades and, although the content morphs with my goals, some things remain constant: pictures of my family sharing time together, of my travel plans (past and future), of my fitness goals, of giving back, and of financial independence.

The wonderful thing about dream boards is that each person's is distinctive and unique, as no two people are the same. As our goals and methods to reach them vary, so do the boards. I have compared our past maps to quilts, and this is a perfectly appropriate item for a dream board, showing how there is no wrong or right way to assemble the pieces that make us whole.

Your board can be as big or as small as you want, and you can display it anywhere you are likely to see it daily.

Make sure it contains images that inspire you and remind you of your own, highly individual good life. Are there locations you love where you dream of living someday? Have you ever read a quote from a public figure that you found particularly inspiring? I currently have "Made to perform" on mine. The people who inspire you to continue your journey to discover a life that is fulfilling and authentic may appear among the images on your dream board.

Don't forget to make it all encompassing: family, friends, romantic interests, pets, fitness, finances and business, lifestyle activities, dream house, car, vacation, accolades for your contribution to your industry, your causes, etc. Print off all the images from the internet and create a montage of your good life.

Goal-Setting

Goal-setting is easy. It's the follow-through that separates the successful people from the masses. Without follow-through, the goal-setting will have lasted no longer than the typical New Year's resolution. According to some researchers, this averages somewhere between three and four weeks after watching the ball drop in Times Square.

The goal-setting and follow-through process—and it is a process, rather than a one-time, set-in-stone-for-eternity event—requires both hemispheres of the brain. Goal-setting for follow-through is multifaceted; it demands both our analytical and visionary skills. Balancing these two seemingly opposing forces is no small task, but when it happens, we are on our way to realizing our dreams.

To capture the mindset needed to set purpose-driven goals, think of a healthy, towering tree. It is deeply rooted in the ground, yet its limbs are flexible enough to withstand the elements. This is how we approach the future. Strong belief in yourself keeps you grounded when the curveballs seem to come out of nowhere and rattle you. Some of these curveballs are societal and even global (pandemics and natural disasters, for example), and others are more personal (think: divorce, layoffs, and illness). Flexibility in life means finding ways to either embrace or work around and through obstacles when it is not possible to move them.

Behavioural scientists have studied goal-setting and attainment for centuries, and they have used logic as well as an understanding of human behaviour (often driven by our emotions) to determine the best way to set goals. A popular acronym for effective goal-setting is SMART. This acronym stands for Specific, Measurable, Achievable, Realistic, and Time Bound. I thought about placing this description in an index or footnote, as I'm sure many of you are familiar with it; however, it is so important I included an overview below. In the chapter "Flipped Upside Right," I'll talk more about goals and include additional strategies.

For now, let's break down SMART:

Specific. Goals must have enough specificity to remain manageable. Without clear definitions of our goals, we run the risk of chasing everything and catching nothing. Boundaries and limits are perfectly appropriate and healthy in certain circumstances, and specificity in goal-setting is one of them. A goal to "be happier" or "exercise more" is so vague it is ineffective in propelling us toward a more fulfilled life. An alternative is, "I will increase my fitness level and create a healthier lifestyle by exercising four mornings a week at my current gym."

Measurable. Like specificity, the ability to measure our goals and the progress toward them is necessary to stay focused. If you decide you want to increase your income, would a 2 per cent increase mean you'd reach your goal? Or should the goal involve improvement in your foreign language skills; perhaps test scores from written and oral exercises could serve as a measurement of your efforts. For our fitness example, you may say, "I will start this process with a personal trainer fitness assessment measuring my strength, BMI, and mobility. I will determine which improvement to target over the next two months. I will then complete a follow-up assessment every eight weeks for the remainder of the calendar year, shifting the targeted progress at each juncture."

Achievable. Wish lists are relatively simple to create; however, determining the steps needed to fulfill your wishes can cause some to feel perplexed. Where to start? In which order should you proceed through the steps? Are you forgetting a step? In assessing how capable you are of achieving your goals, you must be realistic. To set a goal to run a marathon next month without training or a past exercise regime isn't realistic. To set this same goal a year out is absolutely within your reach. A big part of achievability also encompasses your resources, determination, and willingness to devote what is required to attain the goal.

Realistic/Relevant. I've seen the R in SMART goals referred to as realistic and/or relevant. When you begin any new goal or dream, big or small, limiting beliefs may try to spoil the fun. There is a danger of telling yourself you are "just being realistic," or "keeping yourself from disappointment," like a well-meaning but hopelessly pessimistic friend. Perhaps the only beliefs you should be permitting here are the ones that tell you the sky's the limit. Now that we have established that, it is important to define that realistically.

A goal to run a marathon can include a training program over a period of time based on your current physical shape. It's realistic for some to make this program twelve weeks while others realistically will need six months or a year. You can't go from high school graduation to becoming a lawyer in three years any more than you can solve world poverty in the short term. However, you can become a lawyer in about seven years and/or you can dedicate as much of your energy as possible to the mission of decreasing the poverty in the world. "Realistic" can be very subjective, and although there are facts that need to play a role in goal-setting, I often think "What would Dolly or Oprah do?" Like I said, the sky's the limit!

Time Bound. As with other areas in the SMART approach, the understanding of your resources plays an important role in your outcome. You need to make decisions around your commitments, and time is by far one of your most precious commodities.

When you set a goal of fitness and training you might ask yourself: Is the time commitment in line with my self-care time allocation? Training for an Ironman triathlon while raising small children and working full time might be a stretch. It might not, if your schedule is so flexible you have time for all three. If it is a stretch, shifting the goal to a sprint triathlon could be an alternative. Every goal requires a finite amount of time to achieve.

Summary

Over time, your goals and your views of them will change, and if you are anything like me, some will do so quite dramatically. This is the case for many people, a welcome indicator of growth and progress. If nothing changes over the decades, internally or externally, are we truly alive? Welcoming and adapting to change is a wonderful way to remind yourself that you are living in a world that never stops turning.

Learning and experiencing what life has to offer can significantly change your views and your priorities in life. Your experiences—the rewarding ones and the less enjoyable ones—become a source of gratitude. They have shaped you into the person you are today, and allow you to look back at your younger self and realize how far you have travelled.

Remind yourself that you made the best decisions you could using the information and the emotional maturity you had at the time. At different junctures in this book, I share different points in my life when my functioning and sense of direction were not at their best. Had I not experienced these periods, I would not be able to tell you with certainty that our beginnings or current situations do not define our future. I'm living proof.

I know this to be true: people can and do start from places of poverty, poor health, and even widespread crisis. Using several tools, including determination and goal-setting, they change their outlook, their situation, and, sometimes, the world around them. It is possible that such trying times are an ideal place to begin the escape plan. Wherever you are in your journey, I encourage you to start designing what comes next.

Dreamin' Bout the Good Life

When I was in my early twenties, life could have gone either way. I was living a dysfunctional life and not one that was sustainable for the long term. I really wanted out, and with a bit of help from the universe, and a lot of reading and learning new life strategies, I turned it around. Enjoy!

DREAMIN' BOUT THE GOOD LIFE

BY GAIL TAYLOR AND MALLORY BISHOP

Way down south in a broke-down house
complete with a leaky ceilin'
I used to party all night then watch the sunrise
an' wake up with a groggy feelin'

Time went by in the blink of an eye
I was searching for a brand-new meanin'
Wanted to turn that house into a beautiful home
and change the way I was feelin'

Starin' at the rich and famous
Why can't I be in their boat?
Thinkin' bout mansions
fast cars, fashion
Where's my luxury coat?

Dreamin' bout the good life
Gonna make it grand
Learnin' all the mind games
for my journey and my plan
I told myself I got this
yeah, it was as good as mine
My future had a roadmap
all I had to do was put the car in drive
Dreamin' bout the good life
Dreamin' bout the good life

Bought a Samsonite just to do it right
Studied all the rich guys' readin'
Built a business tall to watch it all fall
but I knew where my path was leadin'

Friends with some rich and famous
invited me for drinks on their boats
Visitin' the mansions in my sports cars
oh, and I bought my luxury coat

Dreamin' bout the good life
gonna make it grand
Learnin' all the mind games
for my journey and my plan
I told myself I got this
yeah, it was as good as mine
My future had a roadmap
all I had to do was put the car in drive
Dreamin' bout the good life
Dreamin' bout the good life

Still lovin' the journey and keepin' my soul
I'm makin' the money while carin' for the world
I'm still...

Dreamin' bout the good life
gonna make it grand
Learnin' all the mind games
for my journey and my plan
I told myself I got this
yeah, it was as good as mine
My future had a roadmap
all I had to do was put the car in drive
Dreamin' bout the good life
Dreamin' bout the good life

CHAPTER THREE

Flipped Upside Right

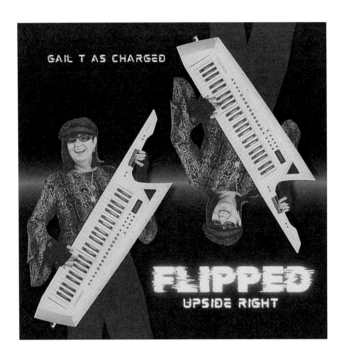

This chapter is focused on understanding passions and purpose and the role they can play when designing your life. I took the approach of sharing my story and describing the tools in the context of work; however, the message I'm sharing with you does not have to be exclusive to your working life. It's transferable and can be used for planning and manifesting hobbies, relationships, projects, and many other areas of your life. Keep an open mind and use your imagination to transfer the message to your story.

My Story

I worked as a financial advisor for about twenty-five years and, most of the time, it was beyond fulfilling. Helping people with their finances made me feel not just productive, but also that I was contributing in a meaningful way. About fifteen years into my career, a small voice in the back of my head started telling me there was something missing, and it was getting louder every day. I wanted to take my work to the next level, to do . . . more?

At the time, I didn't know what *more* meant, exactly. However, I suspected it centred on growing my practice in the corporate sense—more clients, more assets to manage, more income. What happened next was not something I could have predicted. I stumbled on a process of discovering how to incorporate my life's purpose into my business and it threw a few curveballs my way. I realized I could level up my commitment to contributing to the world being a better place in ways I could not have imagined.

It all started when I decided to hire a business coach, hoping for guidance, and it was his insights that caused me to rethink the direction of my professional life. The coach began by saying, "Tell me about Gail Taylor and tell me about your practice. What are you trying to get out of it and life?"

"That's easy. I want to work with my clients to help them create their financial independence so they will be able to retire and enjoy life. I also want to create my own financial independence so that I can sell my practice and go on to do more philanthropic or volunteer work. I want to make the world a better place." (Yes, I know. I would have made a perfect beauty pageant contestant.)

"Gail, that's not how it works," he said. "You don't work until you can retire in order to then live your purpose and passion in life. You've got to find a way to incorporate your passion into your work *now*. If you can't do that, you might as well sell your practice and move on."

Having been a student of peak performance for so many years, I realized instantly that he was offering me valuable advice. Although my work was meaningful and exciting, it wasn't fulfilling my life's purpose on the highest level.

My coach gave me many different exercises to do as my "homework." In the process, I discovered responsible Investing. *Environmental, Social,* and corporate *Governance* investing (ESG) means screening out and not investing in companies that harm the planet and its inhabitants.

Starting with the **environmental side,** it was a bit tricky, as we moved further into the understanding of climate change and fossil fuels. I live in Edmonton, Alberta, Canada, a province whose economy relies on the oil industry, so I made the decision at the time not to completely screen out this industry. I did, however, add some investment criteria, and focus on investing in companies that were working at: having a neutral carbon footprint; spending research and development dollars on alternative energy for the future; and developing alternative ways to clean up residue in hazardous areas like the tailing ponds.

On the **social side**, I was screening out companies that engaged in unethical activities like sweatshops in developing countries. It was important to me to avoid businesses that hired local criminals to intimidate people into working long hours without proper breaks or pay.

On the **governance side**, an example would have been a diverse board of directors. Were there women on the board? People with different ethnic backgrounds?

What really appealed to me about ESG investing was that it took a big-picture approach. Profits still mattered; however, now we were looking at *stakeholder theory* versus *shareholder supremacy. It became about the triple bottom line: profit, people, and the planet.*

Once I discovered ESG and all the investment availability in the sector, it was a gamechanger. It allowed me to live on purpose with a passion that gave my work meaning beyond personal satisfaction. I crunched the numbers and learned that being globally conscious was going to be an option, because the client's return would be the same. Discovering that it was possible to look after the planet *and* earn healthy returns gave my work a new dimension. I will say these returns were largely due to my conservative practice managing people's retirement portfolios. I changed the tagline of my practice to "creating my clients' wealth while strengthening the world."

Once I was committed to making the change, the next step would be to approach my clients. I did not know what to expect. They did not hire me to be a "do-gooder," so I was at risk of losing clients and reducing the size of my practice. At the time, I was managing about eighty million dollars, and I was prepared to see a decrease down to sixty-four million. I had anticipated this cut of approximately 20 per cent, and although it meant my income would decrease significantly, I was prepared to accept these consequences. I felt strongly about this change and braced myself for the possibility of a loss. As it turned out, it was as if I'd swung at the curveball and sent it sailing over the fence. Instead of a loss, my business grew. When I approached my clients about it, they embraced it with positive and empowering reactions.

Clients impressed me by asking, "Why didn't you bring this to us sooner?" Overall, it was an amazing context shift within my practice. Several years later, I was managing $130 million and was not only able to sell my practice for a premium value, but also make it a positive transition for my clients and my amazing partners that took over. That was an incredible learning experience for me: talk about gamechangers and powerful tools! Without even realizing the far-reaching effects it would have, by hiring a business coach, I learned how to pivot to a life with purpose. I was now deeply committed to work that was meaningful to me.

I have a deeply held conviction that you should be working at a place and in a job that you're passionate about. You spend half your waking hours at work (sometimes more). The story above shows how I did it without changing my job title or company. I'm hoping you can achieve a similar shift, in a way that works for you. It's also important to consider that a job that might be the ideal fit for you could be a horrible, draining job for another person.

A great example of this involves my son's current position. He recently took on a role at an extermination company. He loves it. He excels in this field. I, on the other hand, would find that job to be my worst nightmare. I am not interested in putting myself anywhere near cockroaches or rats or bed bugs, but those little critters don't bother him. Being able to remove them so people can enjoy peace of mind and feel comfortable in their homes is something that he's good at and proud of, so everybody wins. What does this mean for you? It is a reminder that there are countless ways to do meaningful work and help others. People have many different skills and talents, which is fortunate, because the world is full of people with different needs. There are people who need help with their medical concerns, their finances, and their legal issues. They need advice in areas ranging from childrearing to estate planning. Our society tends to equate certain jobs with more prestige than others, yet there is value in every job that meets a legitimate need. As impressive as a neurosurgeon's skills may be, if you have uninvited rodents in your home, this is not the person for that task.

I think it would be incredible for you, if you are unhappy with your current employment situation, to consider a pivot, either like me with the same position, or a new role in its entirety. Consider spending the required time and energy looking for an alternative that would give you similar hours, pay, and benefits, and would give you a more rewarding opportunity. You're worth it! WHY SETTLE?

In the remainder of this chapter, let's look at some tools designed to help those of you searching for your purpose and create a path toward fulfilling it.

Tools for Thought

Let's start with not settling for a job simply because it is "good enough." Refrain from telling yourself you could always do worse. Staying with a job solely because it was adequate at one point (possibly years ago) is not a compelling reason to remain in that position.

There may be a good reason for feeling stuck or limited at a job that once seemed exciting: you have grown. As a child, you outgrew your clothes and shoes, sometimes more often than your parents might have been able to afford, but you did grow. When you reached adulthood, you continued to grow in ways that are every bit as important. Being restless at your job is like your toes poking through the tip of your shoes. It's a welcome sign that you are ready for the next chapter in your life.

You can create a work environment that fills you with enthusiasm and challenges you in exciting new ways. If it exists, you can find it. If it does not exist, why not create it? No one can do this for you. Your growth is your responsibility, and few things are more rewarding than stretching yourself and taking risks you are ready to take. Remember, the process of living with purpose begins in your mind.

Purpose and Passion in the Goal - GET

I use the "GET" approach as a tool. I learned this initially from Napoleon Hill and then again from Tony Robbins. I call it the "GET." It stands for goals, emotions, and to-dos. Once you zero in on your purpose, "GET" is a tool to help align your thoughts, emotional buy-in, and actions.

GET continues to guide me through the process of creating many of my life's goals. If you are a student of peak performance, you surely have come across this exercise in personal-growth books, and I hope you have found it as rewarding as I have. It takes time to master the "GET" tool, because the work involved in preparing and executing your strategy can be quite significant; however, so is the reward. You can begin by imagining what your dream job looks like. Is it anything like what you are doing now? Does your current job simply need tweaking, or do you need a completely different arena?

I use this tool to create my strategies in many different areas of my life. It's not exclusive to job creation; in fact, it is a powerful goal-setting tool regardless of the goal. If you have any life challenges or activities that you're currently working on, try using the "GET" strategy.

Here is a sample blueprint:

In a statement form you might start with:

I would love to be a (job description or title) because this role aligns with (a need/want of mine). Each day would be (positive descriptive word or phrase) and (positive descriptive word or phrase).

Some possible examples:

I would love to be a **real estate agent** because this role aligns w**ith my wish to help people find homes they enjoy and can afford**. Each day would be **different, presenting new challenges** and **it would give me personal satisfaction to hand people the keys to their new home.**

Or

I would love to be a **personal trainer** because this role aligns with **my desire to help people lead healthier lives.** Each day would be **a chance to help my clients understand they have the power to keep themselves fit.**

Or

I would love to be a **CPA** because this role aligns with **my love of keeping financial information in order.** Each day would be **an opportunity to help others understand exactly how much money they are earning and spending, and this will help them with good financial decisions.**

Remember, not everyone is suited to, or desirous of, the same role. Reading some of these examples, it might be difficult for you to imagine finding fulfillment in any of these jobs. That's because you are attracted to things that line up with *your* values and what is important to *you*. Values are unique to you, as is your life journey to honour them.

Consider such luminaries as Mahatma Gandhi or Nelson Mandela or even Mother Teresa. Their values and their day-to-day goals were very different from mine. One of my values centres around emotional well-being, and I'm not only a bit of an adrenaline junkie, I also love to have fun. I like laughing, I like smiling, I like giggling, and it is very important to me that each day has some of these elements in it.

The three people above were dedicated to changing "the rules of the game." They fought to change the game itself and changed the course of history in the process. We admire these "gamechangers," because they sacrificed and focused on these life-and-death matters, things that had nothing to do with giggling.

I am not downplaying my values by highlighting these amazing people. Everyone has their own unique emotional responses and what gives us a sense of fulfillment varies from person to person. It is your job to do you, and to figure out your values and purpose.

The aspiring CPA in our example above might find the physical work of a trainer exhausting. The person who hopes to be a personal trainer might be bored to tears looking at balance sheets. I encourage you to devote time to examining what is important to you and not to anybody else. What do you like doing? Are you a gamer? Are you a golfer? Are you a giver? There are several online personality profile tests, like Myers-Briggs, you can take that result in providing you with a list of jobs or careers that align with your inner core.

Just to remind you, we are still in the G of the "GET" strategy. After you have developed a clear definition of the role that would be the right fit for you, next comes determining where this role exists. There are different ways to approach this. One is to start with some online research and make a list of all the organizations you feel would hire people for the position for which you are searching. The situation of a personal trainer role has many options, some of which are gyms, retirement homes, and cruise ships. Use your imagination and let your values and lifestyle goals be your guide. You could then search these companies' websites and find the career opportunity section. Look at the job descriptions. What qualifications do you need to get this job? What qualifications are desired but not required? What type of education does this position require? Some jobs will help you with further education and training should you possess the essential skills for the position. Check out the compensation and make sure it is in line with your expectations. Once you have completed these tasks, use the information from your lists and write the goal out as a final statement or paragraph using all the SMART measures outlined in the previous chapter.

Here's an example of one of my goals:

To build and operate a successful business until January 2, 2031 (my seventy-fifth birthday, when I will re-evaluate). The business will be broken into three components:

- A recorded music catalogue in excess of thirty songs
- Keynote presentations encompassing several topics of personal growth with delivery of a minimum of twelve per year
- A merchandise line, including inspirational pendants and a personal growth book (which you are reading), all of which will be sold to inspire, uplift, trigger, and be constant reminders to others to follow through to create the life they want.

Once you define your version of the above example, you are ready to put together a list of resources you *have* and a list of resources you will *need*. Do not underestimate the advantages you already have. Your talents and abilities are the building blocks of accomplishments that move your entire world forward.

Some examples:

Let's do a skills inventory along with your personal strengths. What are your:

- Technical skills?
- Life skills?
- Social skills?
- Personality strengths?
- Networks of friends and family (list them)?
- Current education?
- Location and its proximity to the resources you need (or the company you want to work for)?

How do you fill the GAPS? What do you need to acquire to attain the role you want:

- Education—you can study online and/or take night courses if you work.
- Skills—define what areas you need to develop and seek out available opportunities to acquire them.
- Money—will you need funds to pay for the above resources or any other aspect of the new role (examples are tools for trades or business clothes for the office)?

As I am fond of saying, *follow-through makes all the difference,* so do not stop making your list after two or three items. *Follow-through* means you have exhausted all possibilities, left no stone unturned. When you commit to following through, doing the minimum is simply not enough. This inventory should include everything that comes to mind. List as many resources as you have and as many as you will need, even if they seem a little far-fetched. It will take some imagination because you may not know yet where and how you will obtain these resources. At this point you are simply listing them. Example number one is the need for education. Education usually requires cash. Are there scholarships available? Is there a family member who would give you a loan?

Having shaped your goals, you can now use the tool to work on something more abstract, but every bit as powerful: emotions. I think this aspect is crucial in living with purpose. The E in GET is emotion.

What will your life feel like if you shift from your current role into this new manifested position? Will you have more time for your loved ones? Will you have more financial resources to be able to take vacations or buy a house or a car? Will you be able to help a family member who is struggling? When you get up in the morning to go to work, will you be looking forward to the day? Will you be excited? Why? What will you be doing that will make you feel so empowered? Focus inward. Does the job make you feel exhilarated?

Emotional buy-in is one of the keys to personal growth. You cannot see or touch emotions; they take up no physical space and yet they strongly influence your search for growth and happiness. You use your emotions as drivers use the instruments on their dashboards. Think of constant stress or anxiety as a "check engine" light coming on. It's telling you your health and vitality need attention.

If you visited my music studio, where I spend several hours a day, you would see my emotional buy-in when you notice the Post-its and signs hanging on my mirror. I often have these pieces of paper to remind me of my *why*. Ask yourself questions related to *your* why. Why are you spending your time and energy as you are? Are your actions in this moment bringing you closer to your goals?

Are you emotionally invested in this life shift you are designing? Although Post-its are useful tools for me, they may not work for everyone. Some people (myself included) find music a wonderful way of putting themselves in touch with their emotions. Songs about overcoming obstacles and rejoicing after accomplishing a goal may lift you emotionally when you are discouraged. Music is known to create dopamine, which gives you a feeling of motivation. The songs at the end of each chapter were written for that exact purpose. Collections of relevant quotes or evocative images may also help you regain focus on your goals. I've previously talked about creating dream boards in depth as they can play a visual role in keeping your motivation alive. Seeing something that helps you remember that you are in pursuit of a concrete, deeply desired outcome is powerful. It puts you in a frame of mind conducive to real progress.

Tools that can help you pursue your purpose are the metaphorical stick and carrot. The "stick" side of not pursuing your dream is something to consider. What will happen if you do not pursue this dream job? What will the result be if you resign yourself to stagnation? Will you stay in a job that you are not really meant to do, arriving home at the end of every day feeling a little burnt out? Why should you settle?

You might convince yourself to take what appears to be the path of least resistance. You may come to doubt your true potential. This sometimes results in your finding yourself in a job you have grown to detest, uncertain of where the pursuit of your dreams was derailed. Avoiding this predicament requires an awareness of both what you are doing and your feelings. Your emotional buy-in keeps you from settling and gives you the strength to go after what you deserve and claim the reward for your investment. I think success in anything is enhanced if you focus on your emotional buy-in.

Successful people manage to follow through even when the current task is difficult. The challenges that you overcome by persevering and completing the task are far outweighed by your successfully getting one step closer to your dreams. Having said that, consider taking the time to start the exercises in this chapter even before you go on to read the next chapter. Once again, I believe that the key difference between successful people and unsuccessful people is follow-through. YOU GOT THIS! FOLLOW THROUGH.

Our work with the GET tool is nearly complete. Once you feel secure about the areas above, it's time to create your to-do list. For some, that's a big ask. Others are wired to live with to-do lists. We all have different personality traits; some of the activities that worked for me are going to be hard for you. Some activities that were hard for me are going to be easy for you. Celebrate your differences; they make great things possible.

A to-do list might look something like this:

- Determine if the required education is available online, when the next program starts, and what the cost will be.
- Look into the requirements for acceptance in the program above and, if transcripts from previous courses are required, contact the institution and obtain them.
- Determine where the financial resources will come from by creating a list of options: perhaps working overtime; taking out

a loan; applying for a scholarship; or tapping into your savings account.

Your list should have several items. It can include items that will take you a day or a couple of weeks, or a couple of years to complete.

You are designing your life, after all! As monumental and intimidating as that may seem, it is also exhilarating. Part of mapping out your future is enjoying the journey. This journey doesn't start when you get hired in this role. The journey starts when you begin doing what is essential to reach your goal. It is so rewarding; you feel a renewed enthusiasm for realizing your purpose. Instead of zapping your energy, these activities should increase it.

If you find yourself heading in a direction you didn't expect, keep in mind that, sometimes, this is the best possible outcome!

Flipped Upside Right

"Flipped Upside Right" is a story about "Living on Purpose." My own adventure was about shifting a *traditional* financial practice to a *socially and environmentally responsible* one. Whatever you are engaged in you can find a way to make it part of your passion or maybe you move on. Enjoy our retro lyric video. It's fun!

FLIPPED UPSIDE RIGHT

BY GAIL TAYLOR AND MALLORY BISHOP

On the building's top floor
she arrived to get hired
She may have lacked skills
but she had a strong desire
In her Hugo Boss suit
wearing confidence galore
she presented a plan
that the man could not ignore

Honoured with clients
and markets that soared
timing was right, success was ensured
but never fulfilled
Something just wasn't right
so she brought in the coach
Next level in sight

Said her job was a stepping stone
to follow her passion
He said living life on purpose
should be her main attraction

Her world was flipped upside right
She could live her purpose
She found a spark to ignite
The challenge was real
it made her feel small
but she knew she could make it
in a way that cared for all
Her world was flipped upside right
Her world was flipped upside right

Yes ESG investing was a new way to go
With help from the people
whose money she'd grow
Embraced the opportunity
Everything felt right
The triple bottom line
with the planet's health in sight

Her job was a stepping stone
to follow her passion
Living life on purpose
could be her main attraction

Her world was flipped upside right
She could live her purpose
She found a spark to ignite
The challenge was real
it made her feel small
but she knew she could make it
in a way that cared for all
Her world was flipped upside right
Her world was flipped upside right

Listen up now
Your world can flip upside right
You could live your purpose
just find a spark to ignite
Our world can flip upside right
We can live our purpose
We'll make a new spark to ignite
The challenge is real
It can make us feel small
but we know we can make it
in a way that cares for all
Let's flip our world upside right
Let's flip the world upside right

CHAPTER FOUR

Let Your Freak Flag Fly

My Story

Research indicates that our environment significantly influences, motivates, and shapes us. As per Jim Rohn's theory, the five individuals we spend the most time with wield considerable influence over our identities. If this theory holds true, then the company we keep, both professionally and personally, holds immense importance. Expanding beyond that circle of influence, my journey has exposed me to meeting a wide spectrum of people, leading me through moments of triumph and turmoil, ultimately shaping the person I am today.

Marriage has been a recurring theme in my life, a journey marked by trials and transformation. I've walked down the aisle four times, each partnership offering its own lessons and challenges. Yet, amidst the complexity, each relationship has contributed to my growth in its own way.

In my youth, I also found myself drawn to what society often labelled as "bad boys," a path intertwined with my struggles against substance abuse. This inclination resulted in some dysfunctional relationships, to say the least. I recall a particular incident with an early boyfriend who exhibited intense jealousy. He forbade me from visiting family out of town, threatening self-harm if I did—a coercive tactic I found deeply unsettling.

My first marriage, entered into at a tender age, ended abruptly amid the discovery of his illegal activities. It was a wake-up call, a realization that the allure of rebellion came at too high a cost.

The subsequent unions were fraught with their own trials. Infidelity shattered the trust in my second marriage, while distance, addiction, and my infidelity strained the bonds of my third. Yet, through each hardship, I gleaned valuable insights about myself and the kind of partnership I sought.

It was in my fourth marriage that I found my soulmate, Harold, a steadfast companion with whom I've weathered life's storms. Together, we've built a life filled with love, enduring through thirty-four years and counting.

Despite societal expectations of lifelong unions, I stand by my decision to seek the right partner, even if it meant enduring heartache along the way. The journey to find true companionship has been a process of trial and error, but one that has ultimately led me to a place of fulfillment and happiness.

Reflecting on my journey, I've come to understand the importance of surrounding myself with individuals who uplift and support me. It's a lesson learned through experience—one that continues to shape my relationships today.

As I continue to evolve, I recognize my own imperfections and strive to address them with humility and grace. Like all of us, I am a work in progress, learning and growing with each passing day.

Sharing this story wasn't easy; it's a testament to some of my mistakes and shortcomings. But I also see it as a testament to resilience and a determination to embrace growth, no matter how challenging the path may be.

Tools for Thought

Other People's Energy and Our Reactions

We are all connected. You began your life enmeshed with others, developing autonomy and hopefully creating healthy boundaries. Despite your valued independence, as poet John Donne reminds us, "No man is an island." That is, very few people live fulfilling lives without connections to others. Instead of needing others for your physical survival, you need them for friendship, intellectual growth, and a sense of community.

Although it may sound like metaphysical mumbo-jumbo, I believe there are energetic connections between you and others that influence your thoughts and moods in ways that are subtle and mysterious. Like bacteria and viruses, your emotions are contagious. Another person's good mood can rub off on you, even when you don't know the person or the reason for their happiness.

My husband Harold loves to laugh and, without question, he has put a smile on so many faces. We worked together for several years and, when he left the firm, I heard over and over from colleagues how much they missed his laughter. Guests staying at our house raved about the lift they experienced from being in the presence of his laughter. It's magical.

Some people are especially sensitive to the energy of others, and they would probably tell you this can feel like both a gift and a curse, depending on the energy. If it is positive, or at least neutral, they can maintain their stability fairly easily. Anger, sadness, and fear are another matter.

Just as you wear protective clothing when exposed to the elements, you can wear a kind of protective cloak against unwelcome energy. Upon realizing someone else's negative mood or behaviour is affecting you, you can make a conscious decision to recognize your separateness from this person and their energy. It is a healthy boundary, and results in your learning not to take the words and actions of others personally.

Emotional Maturity

Humans come into this world very self-centred, and, yes, that includes you. Your challenge, and sign of growth, is understanding that not everything is about you. This can be reflected in your learning to refrain from taking the actions and words of others as directed at you personally. It really isn't about you.

People come in all shapes, sizes, and personality types. How talkative, shy, comical, serious, or silly any given person is will vary. Your mood and behaviour will also vary for any number of reasons. When someone interacts with you (pleasantly or not), it is not necessary to conclude that this person treats you this way because of your personal qualities. This person may treat most people this way. Again, it really isn't (all) about you.

It is also possible that a person's demeanour could be very different on different occasions. This person's mood and behaviour could be attributed to many other causes: fatigue, personal issues, job stress, or hunger. When you refuse to take another person's words and actions personally and see them for what they are—their own material, not yours—you free yourself. You can then choose how you respond to others. You can engage in debates and discussions of your opinions, but this is a choice, not a requirement. Other people are separate from you. You can create boundaries and connections as you wish.

Another key point about separateness here involves your opinions. Your feelings and preferences are a part of who you are, not the beginning or end of your identity. Whether you realize it at the time, you are presented with an opportunity to grow emotionally every time you interact with others. These interactions can be functional, dysfunctional, or just plain strange. You can show that you have developed a certain level of self-awareness when you realize that you can agree to disagree. You can befriend a person and not necessarily agree with all their beliefs.

This is not the only time self-awareness proves to be a useful tool. When I think about my own emotional maturity, I go back to the place in my journey not so long ago when I challenged others in the workplace to function in an environment that wasn't always conducive to their traits. I pledged to myself to never again cause such angst.

Self-Awareness

Self-awareness is the ability to perceive yourself as a unique individual. It is the recognition that you have separate thoughts and feelings and can act independently of others. Thinking about yourself is not just acceptable, it is advisable. It helps you relate to others in a constructive way. When you are self-aware, you are observing yourself and you are evaluating how your words and actions affect others. This is unlike thinking only about yourself, which is being self-absorbed. It is not a good look on anyone over three years of age.

Your self-awareness grows in complexity as you mature, because you also develop an awareness of how others see you. You can allow it to be painful hearing that others perceive you as lacking in some way or not fitting in, something many young people want desperately. I was learning to sing at the beginning of my music journey and, after two years, I realized I didn't have a natural talent, and it was going to require a lot of work and practice to develop a sound that I liked. I made the decision to go another way and hire vocalists to sing my songs and I concentrated on my songwriting.

I think writing became my super strength because I talk so much, and songs are just stories turned into lyrics. When I commented on my voice to a few of the producers I was working with, I received a compliment about my self-awareness. "You're right, lady—you can't sing well enough to record." I'm paraphrasing in a tongue-and-cheek manner, but you get my point. Understanding (and accepting) yourself—warts, and all—is a gamechanger. It allows you to plan that next step in designing your own life.

Looking at yourself on a macroscale and within your current environment also plays a role. Our societal notions of gender are especially relevant to many people today. Social media facilitates discussion about who we think we are and how the world sees us in terms of traditional and restrictive gender roles.

In the twentieth century, the civil rights and women's movements, among others, encouraged you to see others as they were: your equals as human beings. At the same time, as marginalized groups found their voices, they expressed a desire for the things the dominant classes may well have taken for granted: the ability to obtain an education and earn a living wage, freedom to define your interpersonal relationships as you chose, and a sense of safety in public and private life.

A debate continues in our society about the way we see ourselves and the way others see us as it relates to gender. Use of personal pronouns is part of this discussion, opening an examination of how language is a part of self-expression.

Growing up in the sixties and seventies was very different from growing up today. No computers, no social media, and somewhat rigid traditions. In grade school I had to wear a dress. Girls were not allowed to wear pants. I was a tomboy, so climbing trees and playing baseball before the bell rang was my jam. My mother was smart enough to suggest I wear capris under my dress and roll them up.

Another indicator that I didn't quite fit the mold was when I took a job for the city of Ottawa as a labourer. I drove a dump truck, cleaned the streets on the midnight shift, and donned my hardhat and construction boots with pride. When I finally landed in my long-term role, in a male-dominated industry, as a financial advisor, it didn't faze me. I fit in. I was as comfortable in the boardroom, often being the only female, as I was in any other environment.

With that backdrop, I don't know what would have happened if I was in today's gender-shifting culture. I was very messed up as a teenager, sometimes with suicidal thoughts, and searching for a way out. I may have just wanted to become a boy. I feel fortunate now that I emerged from this challenging and hormonal time as I am very comfortable with my gender and believe I am in the perfect place for me.

Seeing the Potential in Others

Awareness of others is the first step in realizing that we all need each other. Living things depend on one another, and humans are no different. We form alliances and groups to work for the betterment of the whole, while serving the needs of ourselves.

You can help yourself and our society by maintaining an awareness of every person's uniqueness. It is often these differences that will inspire you to make a difference of your own. Recognizing and praising people's gifts, be they for effective communication, fair treatment of others, or simply the ability to make you laugh, benefits everyone.

It is more than simply a nice gesture to acknowledge the talents and abilities of others; it is the fuel that can give them the energy needed to reach the next level. You don't need religion or politics or even big-picture thinkers to remind you that every person matters, that your actions can have far-reaching, powerful effects on many, many people.

We all win when we help others make the most of their gifts, on both an individual and societal level. What is society, really, but a group of individuals? The possibilities for growth and improvement are endless, and there is nothing to lose. While some of your resources, like time and money, may be limited, your ability to lift others up is not. Elevating another person benefits you just as much, if not more. When we help one another to become our best selves, ultimately we create space for people to reach for a better world for us all.

I've had the honour over the years to engage in the above philosophy. I try so hard to live my truths and, although I sometimes get it right, I've made big mistakes. One mistake resulted in the challenges some had working with me, as my expectations were very high and, I'm embarrassed to say, I unintentionally made others cry. To any of you reading this, I apologize.

I remember once, when I was in my role as a financial advisor, my manager said to me, "Stop being so nice and so mean at the same time." I rewarded others over the top for hard work and frustrated them over the top when things weren't working.

I've shared my shortcomings to hopefully help you identify that you, like me, have made mistakes and will make more. You are a work in progress and always will be. However, you're not defined by your worst moments and celebrating your successes is also an important part of self-awareness. I'm proud to say I also succeeded in having life-changing positive influences on other work colleagues. I hired a very talented young man from Uganda who was new to Canada, which resulted in an opportunity for him to build a career in finance and live up to his amazing potential. I also mentored a female colleague out of an assistant-level role into that of a financial advisor, where she so rightfully belonged. I honestly believe that if you can mentor others and help them see their full potential, you will attract an energy to yourself that is magical.

CHOOSING YOUR PEOPLE—including models and mentors

In a perfect world, you would perceive other people's outstanding qualities, absorb and reflect their positive energy, and elevate our society to exhilarating levels. In a perfect world! This happens in the real world when you get in touch with your ability to accept and elevate yourself and others.

With the understanding that you have the power to decide who is welcome in your life and who is not, you can prevent people and environments that exhibit harmful behaviour from threating your ability to live your best life. You can define a harmful situation as one that leaves you feeling deflated and drained rather than elevated.

Part of the reason you might allow this often verbal harmful behaviour around you, even when you are aware it is harmful, is because the people delivering these words often insist that they are "just trying to help." They're not trying to bring you down with their negative assessments and predictions of failure, they are "telling it like it is." Someone must bring you down to earth when you start talking about unpredictable things like passion and dreams and uniqueness.

There is also a critical piece of information to remember when dealing with verbally harmful behaviour from others: you cannot change them. They must do that for themselves, if and when they are ready. When you encounter verbally harmful behaviour from people close to you, there is often a temptation to undertake a mission to fix the toxicity. It is a waste of time.

Your power to make the decision to leave verbally harmful people and situations behind is an act of kindness toward someone deserving: you. In choosing this path, you are creating space in your life for people who inspire and admire you. The people who want success for you as much as you want it for them and for yourself are the ones who are worth your time and energy.

Over the years, I learned to share a significant component of my time with like-minded people that are designing their own lives and manifesting their dreams. In the entertainment business, I spend a lot of time on Zoom calls with several business friends and acquaintances from across Canada and the United States (lots of Nashville folks). When the video call is finished, I walk away feeling empowered. Whether I learned something, shared something, or collaborated on a project, the result is a bounce in my step and an elevated feeling. If I don't have enough going on, I use my crazy imagination and watch a YouTube interview with one of my role models. Spending the afternoon with Paul McCartney or Billy Joel does wonders for my emotional state.

In my forties and fifties, I was fortunate enough to have the role of trustee on many different charity boards, including hospitals, mental health foundations, and international causes. The people on these boards were the epitome of positive energy. They were there to help make the world a better place and often were high-functioning philanthropists, businesspeople, and professionals. Talk about role models.

Now, what about family? There is a saying that you can choose your friends, but you can't choose your family. What you can choose is how much time you are going to spend with the people that drain you. I have an amazing family and with the whole group at Christmas it becomes about forty people. Some of them are my best friends and others I see once a year. You choose what works for you and what allows your strength to shine, not diminish.

Remember, I opened this chapter with Jim Rohn's theory—the idea that the five individuals you spend the most time with wield considerable influence over your identity. Who are you spending your time with?

Let Your Freak Flag Fly

The inspiration for "Let Your Freak Flag Fly" came from my love for change, our current landscape of getting to know ourselves, and making choices about who we are. I love that our journeys as humans evolve with each generation, and it is so cool that we are now diving deeper into figuring out our own identities and stepping into our truths in a more authentic way. In life, I, like many others, was a bit of a misfit., a tomboy in a time when girls HAD to wear dresses to school and a city girl in a family of country enthusiasts. I had the privilege of giving myself permission to be different so I might enjoy my life to its fullest, but many folks don't find that so easy for a multitude of reasons. I wrote this song to encourage everyone to find acceptance within themselves, to love themselves. Don't worry about the people that don't get you. . . . Surround yourself with those that accept you for who you are and let go of the notion that everyone is going to get you. We are human, after all, so I say, "Live and let live!" Oh, and don't forget to let your freak flag fly.

LET YOUR FREAK FLAG FLY

BY GAIL TAYLOR AND MALLORY BISHOP

She's a tomboy
he's into fashion
but they both love glitter
and they both slay dragons
She's the breadwinner
he's the stay home dad
but together they will make
the family they never had
Oh yeah

I'm the kite
gliding through the sky
'cause he's holding to the string
and he loves to watch me fly
There's a tattooed bouncer
an onstage queen
We gotta rock with both of them
to party in the scene

Doesn't matter, I'll go my own way
It ain't easy being different but it is okay

To let your freak flag fly
Go ahead and let your light shine bright
Baby, be too much
I'm gonna sing my song, you better strut your stuff
Let's turn it up loud 'cause we got soul
If they don't understand then we'll just let 'em roll
and let our freak flag fly
Freak flag fly

If the road's not right I'll make my own
There's no wrong turns if I'm living in the zone
They're just road bumps
they'll come and go
Live your best life
You're the star of your own show

Doesn't matter, I'll go my own way
It ain't easy being different but it is okay

To let your freak flag fly
Go ahead and let your light shine bright
Baby, be too much
I'm gonna sing my song, you better strut your stuff
Let's turn it up loud 'cause we got soul
If they don't understand then we'll just let 'em roll
and let our freak flag fly
Freak flag fly
Yeah

Not everyone can handle our light, shine anyway
You be you and I'll be me, we'll shine anyway
We weren't cut from a pattern
and we may have broke the mold
We don't fit in, so stand out
Let's forget what we're told

Let our freak flag fly
Go ahead and let your light shine bright
Baby, be too much
I'm gonna sing my song, you better strut your stuff
Let's turn it up loud 'cause we got soul
If they don't understand then we'll just let 'em roll
and let our freak flag fly
Freak flag fly
Let our freak flag fly
Freak flag fly

CHAPTER FIVE

Ambition's Not a Four-Letter Word
Understanding Your Finances

GAIL T AS CHARGED

If you already have your financial house in order or are well-versed in personal finance and investment strategies, this chapter may validate your choices or help you discover beneficial alternatives. For those of you struggling with or new to financial responsibilities, you're going to love this. This section is dear to my heart. It's simple, it's important, and it can be a gamechanger.

My Story

For me, achieving financial success was synonymous with leading a fulfilling lifestyle. It encompassed indulging in luxuries such as flying business class, acquiring high-end attire, cruising in a sports car, relishing fine dining experiences, luxuriating in five-star accommodations, contributing to philanthropic causes, helping with family support, and investing in business ventures. I felt as though I had ascended to paradise when I reached the top 5 per cent of earners in Canada. This lofty goal was born during a period of unemployment, with only a high school education and lacking connections.

I was in my early thirties when I acquired the role of financial advisor. The previous business my husband Harold and I started, Corey Properties, had to be closed because of some changes in legislation that resulted in decreased client value in our investment propositions. We decided to relocate to Edmonton, Alberta, in order to successfully sell all of the units and take our investors out with a profit.

As Harold embarked on that journey, I started a new career as a commissioned salesperson in a commercial and investment real estate firm and commenced selling small apartment buildings and small retail strip malls. The purchasers were predominantly professionals in the accounting and legal professions, as well as entrepreneurs building real estate portfolios.

A few years into this role, I had an opportunity to work on a property listing, a significantly larger retail mall, with my manager. This meant the purchaser was likely to be a small pension fund or an investor of this calibre. I decided to enroll in the Canadian Securities course to determine how the potential buyers invested the balance of the portfolios they managed. This course contained extensive information on all areas of market and economic events impacting investment performance, including an in-depth overview of such financial instruments as fixed income, equities, derivatives, mutual funds, and exchange traded funds.

I enrolled so it would give me better insight during the negotiation process. It didn't take long into my new studies for me to realize that I would love to shift from selling investment real estate to stocks and bonds. The biggest difference was that real estate sales were very transactional, while investment advising was focused on relationships. When a new client decides to transfer their investments to your firm and allows you to manage their portfolio, you keep them for decades, helping them develop their financial plans and partnering with them through any financial challenges. This had my name all over it.

I loved working with clients and getting to know them, hearing the stories about their families, their work, and their life's journey. I was honoured to help them determine when and how to retire in the style they wanted. When I first decided that this was the route I was going to take, I made a list of all the full-service brokerage houses in the city and sent each one a letter. I explained I had decided to shift from being an investment broker in commercial real estate to an investment broker in securities and was looking for the opportunity to interview with their firm. I further explained in the letter that the goal for the interview was to determine whether I could add value to their team of financial advisors and also whether their structure would be beneficial to my requirements (win/win).

As you might recall from the last chapter, I mentioned it was a male-dominated industry. This didn't affect me once I was hired; however, getting in the door was a bit challenging. After several interviews with 100 per cent male managers, the offers fell short of what I hoped to accomplish. They kept offering me a position as an administration or marketing assistant for one of the male advisors. I finally stumbled upon a firm that was willing to take a chance on a female advisor. I had several interviews with the firm's manager and assistant manager over a two-week period just before the Christmas holidays. I had promised myself I would find my new role before January 1, 1993, so I was relentless. I called every day to ask for the position. Eventually, my persistence paid off and I was offered a position as a financial advisor commencing in the new year. I was very fortunate in this new role as I attracted a manager that remained in his role through my entire tenure and, without a doubt, was a mentor, role model, and an integral part in my success.

I started my new role in January of 1993. As a financial adviser, you have the autonomy to build your own practice. You spend your own money on marketing, you determine what type of clients you would like to attract and what type of investments you're going to recommend, and you build your own business plan. You're running your own business within the infrastructure of your employee brokerage house.

After the initial training session and interviewing ten of the top advisors in the firm, I determined that I was going to model the areas they all incorporated. This consisted of managing conservative retirement portfolios and completing comprehensive financial plans with every client.

These financial plans could then be reviewed and updated on an annual basis, allowing us to monitor and make sure they were aligned with their goals. It was a great honour to work in this role for twenty-five years.

During that time, I participated in many public-speaking opportunities, from talking at conferences to my peer group, to private seminars for investors, to teaching "Introduction to the Financial Markets" at the University of Alberta.

I'd like to spend the remainder of this chapter sharing some of that information, including basic financial strategies that will hopefully help you with some of your financial decisions. After all, if we are going to live our best lives, this includes having our financial houses in order.

Tools for Thought

As we embark on a time when DIY investing is trending, I think it's even more crucial to understand the variables around establishing a healthy financial footing, including planning and investing. I'll start at the beginning.

Personal Budgeting

Our lives are multifaceted in the twenty-first century, and this is reflected in our finances and the budgets we create to manage them.

Plenty of templates for budgets are available online and they contain items such as student loan payments; internet/technology; childcare; pet care; medical, car, and homeowner's insurance; et cetera. You have a lot of information, which can be quite challenging to manage without using a budgeting system. I highly recommend you find the right budget tool that works for you and keep track of the money needed to fund your best life. These templates allow you to track where you are currently spending your money, giving you an awareness and clear picture of exactly what you are doing with your money at this juncture. They will also feed into the next step of determining what shifting you might do to improve your situation to line up with your goals.

The out-of-sight, out-of-mind philosophy doesn't usually work with personal finance. Keeping your finances in order gives you a sense of control over a key resource. When you have developed a habit of reviewing your finances at least monthly, that knowledge puts you in a position of power. You realize that you are in charge of your money, and not vice versa. I know some of you may worry and stress over this area of your life and, I assure you, paying attention to it has the potential to minimize and not exaggerate those feelings.

Living within Your Means

As much as this book celebrates and even encourages optimism regarding finances, it is important for you to understand what living within your means really entails. The definition is easy: DON'T SPEND MORE MONEY THAN YOU MAKE! That raise or new job you are working toward may very well happen soon, but spending money you do not have in hand yet does not usually work when designing your best life. There are exceptions regarding major purchases like your first car or a new home. Having said that, you should focus on paying off the loan and mortgage as soon as possible and stay away from the temptation of retail therapy or vacations that require borrowing. There are many ways to reward yourself without breaking the bank: biking, hiking, camping, walks in nature, listening to music, or having friends over for board games, to name a few.

Home Ownership

A home is without a doubt the biggest purchase many people will make in their lives. It is also a bit of a hybrid in your financial story as it plays a role as both an investment and a personal use item. Your home will most likely increase in value over time. Selling it usually brings in a large sum of money from the equity accumulated from the increased value as well as the equity created from paying off your mortgage.

If owning a home makes sense for you, it will require both long- and short-term planning and a clear understanding of the expenses associated with home ownership, such as mortgages, property taxes, and a number of other variables. If you are considering a condominium, know what the condo fees are and what they cover. Be sure you understand special assessments that might require an unexpected cash outlay.

My recommendation is that you avoid shortcuts. Make sure you have a proper home inspection and a clear understanding of your future costs. There are a lot of options to make sure you cover all your bases, which could include doing your own research, working with real estate professionals, getting advice from an experienced family member, or talking it over with your financial advisor—or maybe a combination of the above. If this is on your dream board, GO FOR IT!

Credit Cards

These financial tools can seem so harmless and so convenient that you can take their availability for granted and sometimes lose track of your spending. I recommend a very conservative approach; if you don't have the cash in the bank to cover the purchase, don't use the credit card. It can be the most expensive debt instrument that exists.

I think you should try really hard to structure your financial well-being by living within your means; however, if life throws curveballs that don't make that possible, bank loans, line of credits, or even second mortgages are far more cost-effective debt instruments than credit cards. Credit card companies often offer cash back and any number of perks to attract your business, but their interest rates can be high enough to cause major financial setbacks.

If you've ever felt a rush when spending using a credit card, you're not necessarily imagining it. A 2021 study from the MIT Sloan School of Management found that credit card spending can activate the reward centres in the brain. It's a bit scary because your brain can allow this little piece of plastic to create an illusion of financial freedom.

The term "shopaholic" describes the person who feels addicted to the high they experience while buying. Being able to afford the items in question should be your criteria for making a purchase. When you need to spend to feel good about yourself, it's time to reassess your priorities. This section is not a condemnation of credit cards. They can be very useful in developing your credit rating, which can serve you well when you embark on a major purchase like a house. Just make sure your choice is to use it, not abuse it. It's for convenience, not debt acquisition. Pay the balance off every month!

Pay Yourself First - The 10 Per Cent Rule

Credit for this phrase goes to George Samuel Clason's 1926 book, *The Richest Man in Babylon*. Finances were less complicated 100 years ago, but many of the guiding principles are the same. The 10 per cent rule is the practice of saving 10 per cent (or a higher percentage, depending on your goals and resources) of your monthly income. Paying yourself first means, when you receive any income, you immediately transfer 10 per cent to your savings or investment account as if it never existed. Then you design your lifestyle; how much is left is what you have to pay the electric bill or stock up on groceries. Making a habit of saving a certain amount of money every month is a good long-term strategy for accumulating your nest egg. Paying yourself first really does work. Another gamechanger.

All the areas above are tools I used over the years to shift into my best life. I didn't always get that part right either and I'm hoping the lessons I learned might help you not make some of the same mistakes I made. I allowed myself to lose sight of my financial well-being and got caught up in the credit card debt web early in my life. My mother bailed me out by paying off all my credit cards and having me pay monthly payments to her until the debt was paid. I was nineteen years old. Don't fret about where you are now. You are where you're supposed to be. It's what you do next that matters.

Having control of the above takes you to the next part of the financial journey. I call it the combination of living for today and planning for tomorrow.

The Basic Financial Plan

Within your plan, you can focus on your future needs and what will help you reach financial independence. The definition of financial independence is usually dynamic and always individualistic. Each person's differences and uniqueness can be determined and incorporated into the definition of a personal financial plan.

Here's the framework: How much would you need to accumulate during your remaining working years to establish a nest egg that would allow you to follow through with your dreams (home ownership, children's education, etc. . . .) while also building the assets required to fund your retirement lifestyle? Now that was a mouthful!

The importance of having a financial plan is multifaceted, including the reality that, for most of you, living on corporate or government pensions is no longer sufficient and therefore not usually a viable strategy. This is in part a result of our living longer than previous generations and changing careers and companies much more frequently.

I'll start this section with an excerpt from the introduction of a book I wrote in 2000, titled *Yes, You Can Have Your Cake and Eat it, Too!* It was the only other book that I wrote and was inspired by my need for a resource to accompany my teachings of my course at the University of Alberta, called "Introduction to the Financial Markets." The book is no longer in circulation, as I wrote it for that specific time, with pertinent information that would no longer be relevant today.

"The investment world is not that complicated. I believe it is perceived to be confusing and mysterious because during our pre- and post-secondary studies we were not taught about investments and because there is a huge unknown component to investing. The unknown exists because none of us has a crystal ball! We cannot definitely know whether interest rates are going up or down, or if the stock market has reached its peak. Having a basic understanding of investment can give you peace of mind and help you stick to whatever discipline you choose, especially during volatile times."

Golf is not that complicated either, but it does require a big-time commitment. Don't underestimate the importance of giving your financial well-being the attention it deserves. If you enjoy spreadsheets and financial markets, become a DIY; if you don't, work with a professional.

Either way, you win if you stay on top of it, one way or another.

The retirement portion of most financial plans begins with your taking a snapshot of where you are now. There are templates available online to help you organize this information. Gather your data and answer this series of questions:

- What dollar amount do you currently have in your tax-free accounts? List the underlying investments.
- What dollar amount do you currently have in your non-tax-free accounts? List the underlying investments.
- Do you own any real estate (including your home and cottage)?
- List any other assets that have not been covered.
- Do you have a pension? What are the details?

- Are you expecting an inheritance you'd like factored into your plan?
- What are your current liabilities (mortgage, consumer debt, etc.)?

Once you have a snapshot of the current assets and liabilities, the next factor in the plan revolves around your lifestyle choices:

- At what age do you want to be in a financial position to be able to retire? In determining this, think about timelines. If you're forty years old and you want to retire at sixty, that means you have twenty years to build the pool of funds that you need to live on for twenty-five to thirty years.
- What do you believe is your life expectancy? A little research will give you the average statistics and then perhaps add in variables like longevity in your family and your lifestyle choices.
- How much of the money you are saving can you comfortably designate to the retirement fund?
- What annual amount do you want to live on in retirement? A rule of thumb is 70 per cent of what you're living on now. It's an interesting percentage because, depending on the age at which you commence building your investment portfolio, 70 per cent of your income equates to 100 per cent, minus the 30 per cent you would have to save to build a nest egg big enough to give you the 70 per cent to maintain the same lifestyle in retirement. Yes, you might have to read that a few times!
- What is your comfort level with risk: high, medium, or low?
- What objectives take priority for you: income, safety, growth, tax advantage, and/or liquidity?

The above is a great starting point to support you in doing your own initial assessment. There will be additional research required on your part to delve deeper into the above areas, including understanding the need for liquidity or the difference between income and growth. Another component to understand is your current asset allocation structure. You can divide your investments into the three main asset classes to determine your diversification. Diversification is a very important part in an investment strategy, so become aware of the percentage of your portfolio that is invested in each of the classes: *cash equivalents, fixed income, and equities.*

Your personal real estate can also be used as a part of your retirement portfolio and can be factored into the cash-flow analysis. One option to achieve this is to sell your residence later in life (perhaps around age eighty) and use the proceeds to live on for your remaining years. Another option is to remain in the home and just finance it through a debt instrument. The most popular available in today's environment is referred to as a reverse mortgage.

Going a bit deeper, I think it's important to develop an understanding of market volatility, as defined by risk tolerance. Would you be willing to watch your portfolio drop 20 per cent and not remove any of the investments, perhaps even buy more because the market is low?

My years of experience as a financial advisor taught me that this can be very hard. When your $200,000 drops to $160,000 or your $20,000 drops to $16,000, and the media is telling you that we are in a financial crisis like nothing we have experienced before, emotional decision-making can take over. I know from experience and a lot of client hand-holding just how challenging this can be. Clients would call me, quite concerned and leaning toward liquidating their entire portfolio to mitigate the risk of further losses. My recommendation would be the opposite: why don't we buy more and bring our average investment cost down?

Another variable is taxation and the importance of structuring your portfolio so that you're paying the least amount necessary.

Don't get me wrong: I am advocating tax advantage, not tax evasion. I really believe in the concept of income tax to cover the development of bridges and highways and hospitals and schools and all the other infrastructure that we have the luxury of experiencing in the Western world. However, I never felt it necessary to pay extra; therefore, I structured my portfolio to maximize the opportunities that were available.

I have given you a very broad brushstroke on the topic of finance as it relates to investments and building a retirement portfolio. I recommend anyone interested in the DIY option keep reading and learning and build a deep understanding of their financial choices.

In my practice, I attracted clients that were not interested in managing their own money. They weren't interested in the time commitment involved in staying on top of the fast-paced and time-sensitive information. It really isn't different from the time commitment to master anything else, from a musical instrument to your golf score. My clients wanted to play golf or vacation with their family during their downtime.

Many young people, perhaps you included, are questioning whether hiring a professional makes any sense with all the focus on how much more you would have if you didn't pay the fee. Here's another way to look at it. Using a professional could easily mean you would net a return higher than the fee. Watch the commercials in reverse. You may have that higher number in your pocket because you didn't do it yourself. If you love managing your money and staying on top of the market, I say do it! If it is taking you away from your passions, delegate it. There is no right or wrong decision here.

Understand Your Investments

Above, I outlined a strategy to assist you in crafting your own financial plan, a roadmap tailored to guide you toward your financial goals.

Consider your financial plan as akin to important legal documents such as your will, power of attorney, or tax returns. You have the option to draft them yourself using templates or software programs, or you can enlist the expertise of a lawyer or accountant. Your decision should be driven by factors like your personality, strengths, and the time you have available.

With financial plans, whichever approach you decide on, there are key aspects of investments that are significant enough for you to take the time to understand.

When investing in public companies, you can loosely categorize them into two groups: blue-chip and speculative. Blue-chip companies, such as established banks in Canada, are considered stable investments with consistent earnings and solid track records. These are typically large-cap companies, making research relatively straightforward when selecting additions to your portfolio. On the other hand, speculative investments involve smaller or start-up companies with potential for rapid growth but also higher risk. While the allure of such investments can be tempting, it's important to acknowledge the associated risks. Personally, I liken investing in speculative stocks to a trip to Las Vegas, preferring to allocate entertainment funds rather than nest-egg dollars.

Investing in any company carries inherent risks; even seemingly stable blue-chip investments can falter, as evidenced by the 2008 financial collapse in the United States (look it up). Diversification is crucial to mitigate such risks. I advise maintaining a portfolio of around twenty companies to ensure that the failure of any single entity doesn't derail your long-term goals. There are also financial instruments like mutual funds that can help you with diversification, especially when you're just getting started.

Here's an overview of some asset classes:

Stocks: Investing in stocks means owning a portion of a company traded on the stock exchange. While your conservative portfolios may hold stocks for five to ten years, monitoring their stability and industry trends is essential. Speculative stocks may require daily or even hourly monitoring, which you might find exhilarating (or not).

Bonds: Investing in government or corporate bonds involves lending money to a company in exchange for fixed returns. Unlike with stocks, bondholders don't become shareholders, they become creditors. Bond values fluctuate with interest rates and are tradable on secondary markets.

Cash equivalents: These short-term interest instruments, with maturity dates of less than one year, serve as liquid assets in portfolios. They include money market instruments and bonds usually issued by various government levels to fund their debts.

Real estate: Real estate investment presents another avenue worth considering. One straightforward approach involves purchasing an apartment, townhouse, or single-family home to rent out for additional income. Holding onto the property over time often leads to capital appreciation, enhancing the investment's success. Alternatively, one can opt to invest in an existing real estate portfolio through a real estate investment trust (REIT).

While the DIY route in real estate investing can be highly profitable, it's essential to recognize the risks and the significant time commitment required for repairs, maintenance, and tenant management. Drawing from my fourteen years of experience in the real estate industry before transitioning to the security sector, I've observed many investors leveraging this asset class to build their robust net worth. The tangible nature of real estate often resonates with investors, offering a perceived straightforward understanding of the market dynamics.

Real estate investments can also provide the opportunity to utilize leveraging through substantial financing. By investing only 25 per cent of the property's value and securing a mortgage for the remaining 75 per cent, investors can access asset values far exceeding their initial cash investment.

So, now that you have an overview, what could go wrong, right?

I mentioned *The Richest Man in Babylon,* written in 1926, and its author's encouragement of investing in what we understand. If something sounds too good to be true, there is a good possibility that it is. Do not allow yourself to be sold the sizzle and not the steak. Knowing what you are investing in or who you are trusting to know on your behalf is essential.

My clients didn't have to understand the stock market. That was my job. They did have to do their due diligence to understand what my level of expertise was, as well as my company's stability and insurance protection levels on their money. Investments always involve a degree of risk, and if you fall prey to a scammer, the chances of recouping the total amount are slim to none. I always bought into the approach that sensible, cautious, and conservative investments can build wealth slowly but surely. Remember the tortoise and the hare when you are tempted by an investment opportunity that seems extraordinarily profitable. Slow and steady win the race.

Allow me to share a few anecdotes from my time in finance to offer some perspective. Nortel was a former Canadian utilities company that expanded its operations in California and went bankrupt in 2013. Its stock experienced a remarkable surge from $20 to $120 per share within a short timeframe, creating numerous millionaires. However, despite this apparent success, the company's financial reports revealed a concerning trend: its earnings lagged behind its expenses, resulting in losses. Moreover, Nortel was involved in questionable practices, including contributing to rolling blackouts in California.

I vividly recall a client reaching out to me, ecstatic that they had purchased Nortel stock at $40, only to see it soar to $100. They asked whether they should sell, to which I responded, "Perhaps I'm not the right person to solicit that advice from, as I would not have recommended the original investment in the first place." Many investors got swept up in the belief that Nortel's growth trajectory would continue unabated, and hesitated to sell their shares.

Another client stands out in my memory. They had acquired Nortel stock through an unsolicited trade in their portfolio managed by me. The value of their investment skyrocketed from $10,000 to $100,000, only to plummet back to zero, without their withdrawing any funds from the account. It's also worth noting that, at the time, Nortel was often perceived as a somewhat blue-chip company, adding to the allure of its stock.

While Nortel epitomized the conservative side of investing, another stock with a tumultuous journey was Bre-X. This Canadian mining company captured headlines in the mid-1990s with grand claims of discovering a gold mine in Indonesia that promised unprecedented yields. They touted it as a venture that would generate immense wealth for all involved, boasting low extraction costs and astronomical returns.

Bre-X experienced a significant stock collapse in 1997. The company's shares were trading at an incredible value before the fraud was uncovered. At its peak, Bre-X shares were trading at over CAD $280 per share. However, following the revelation of fraudulent practices in its gold mining claims, the stock price plummeted to essentially zero. Investors who held onto their Bre-X shares lost their investment.

During this era I witnessed extraordinary stories unfold. I recall hearing about an investor employed as a bus driver investing $10,000 in Bre-X, only to sell before the fraud was discovered. He divested from his Bre-X position when it was valued at two million dollars, generating unimaginable wealth. However, for others, the euphoria soon turned to despair as the truth emerged—Bre-X was a massive fraud. When trading in the company was halted and industry due diligence completed, the stock value dropped to zero. Many investors, caught up in the frenzy, saw their entire investment vanish overnight. Trading in Canadian dollars the stock price of Bre-X rose to $280 per share by 1997 and at its peak it had a market value equal to US$4.4 billion, equivalent to US$8.4 billion in 2023.

The saga of Bre-X unfolded like a gripping TV drama. Shockingly, one of the company's owners and purported engineers met a tragic end when he was allegedly thrown from a helicopter en route to the mine, resulting in his death. The hysteria surrounding Bre-X also fueled speculation in other small mining stocks. These penny stocks experienced wild swings, with prices doubling from $0.45 in the morning to $0.90 in the afternoon, offering investors seemingly irresistible returns.

I've recounted these rather extreme situations to underscore that investing isn't always straightforward. During the US financial collapse in 2008, even conservative equity portfolios saw significant drops, some as much as 35 per cent over an eighteen-month period. These stories aren't meant to discourage you from investing, but rather to highlight that investing is not a science, and it helps to be aware that there is unpredictable human behaviour and psychology involved. My own portfolio remains invested in the asset classes we've discussed. Over time, they've provided me with financial independence and stability that align with my goals.

Ambition's Not a Four-Letter Word

Ambition is not a character flaw, and it doesn't matter if you're an entrepreneur and it's centred around financial success, or if you're a gardener striving for the prize-winning rose. This song was inspired by my own journey and that of others feeling flawed because we wanted more. Remember, your unique aspirations for success are valid and don't reflect any shortcomings in you.

AMBITION'S NOT A FOUR LETTER WORD

BY GAIL TAYLOR AND MALLORY BISHOP

They claim to know what's good for you
Which track they wish you'd take
But your empire is yours to build
don't let them hold much stake

There's nothin' wrong with a picket fence
or a day-to-day routine
But it's also cool to make your own rules
and dream a bigger dream

If it fills your heart, then sing it
believe it to achieve it

Embrace your ambition
you don't need permission
just keep movin' along
It's not a character flaw to reach for a star
or decide where it is you belong
Follow your bliss, I am tellin' you this
You may think it's absurd
But a dream is not a mousetrap, baby
and ambition's not a four-letter word

Who stands to gain if you want more
You can't dim others' light
Why leave big changes to the stars?
It's your story to write

If it fills your heart, then sing it
believe it to achieve it

Embrace your ambition
you don't need permission
just keep movin' along
It's not a character flaw to reach for a star
or decide where it is you belong
Follow your bliss I am tellin' you this
You may think it's absurd
But a dream is not a mousetrap, baby
and ambition's not a four-letter word

We've all been conditioned to follow the pack
But when you follow your heart, there's no goin' back
No one can stop you if you lean into it
just do what you do 'cause you love to do it

Embrace your ambition
you don't need permission
just keep movin' along
It's not a character flaw to reach for a star
or decide where it is you belong
Follow your bliss I am tellin' you this
You may think it's absurd
But a dream is not a mousetrap, baby
and ambition's not a four-letter word

PART TWO

LIFE ON THE INSIDE

As we transition into Part Two, it might be a good juncture to remind you that your journey is what I refer to as "the game of life" and that you are in the exact place you should be. Staying where you are or taking on massive change is a decision that you make based on what's working for you and what's not. I'm reminded of the expression: "How's that working out for you?"

CHAPTER SIX

You and You Alone

My Story

As a child, I remember having the propensity to create opportunities seemingly out of thin air. My thinking might have been a bit unconventional, or what we would describe today as "out of the box." I had an instinct for seeing possibilities and opportunities in any curveballs coming my way. Over the years, I was able to develop this ability into a tool that served me well.

As I write this book, I'm dealing with a situation that falls into this category. It was January of this year (2024), and I was headed back home to Edmonton from Ottawa. The morning of my departure, I packed, inserted my contact lenses, and began driving to the airport. Watching the road, I kept finding myself distracted by a dark blob in the middle of my field of vision. Was something stuck to my contact lens? Was it dirt? It looked like a blurry blob— pear shaped with a line streaking out behind it.

Once I reached the airport, I removed my contacts; however, the blob remained front and centre, no matter where I looked. I contacted my optometrist and explained the situation. She asked if I could come to her office that afternoon. I explained that I was at the Ottawa airport and flying home that day; however, I could see her the following day.

Sitting in her examining room, I explained with my tongue-in-cheek attitude that it seemed like there was a piece of sperm in my eye, or perhaps a tadpole. It was annoying and somewhat alarming, and it was permanently housed in the centre of my right eye's field of vision.

The doctor performed several tests, including imaging, trying to find an explanation for my ocular stowaway. She smiled as she showed me the tiny object on the image and informed me that it wasn't my imagination, that it did resemble a spermatozoon. She explained that she was initially concerned that it was a more serious issue and that possibly something from my retina had detached; however, she had good news.

The blobs were what optometrists refer to as "floaters." A floater is a small amount of gel that detaches from the back of the eye. Floaters move around in our eyes and, for the most part, they are harmless. She explained it would probably go away within a few months, as it would most likely just dissipate or fall to the bottom of my eye. I thanked her and left the office, relieved but still unsure.

As I was driving home, watching the blob and the road simultaneously, I realized I had some choices about how I was going to deal with this . . . uninvited guest. From my mental tool kit, I chose one of my favourites: imagination. I decided to nickname this passenger "Spermboy." If Spermboy was going to be freeloading in my eye for the next month or so, I would put him to good use.

Every time I noticed Spermboy, I would remember that I really wanted to focus on my fitness that month. Rather than let him frighten me or annoy me with his constant presence, I decided he could help me with something I was working on: training for my upcoming bike trip through France, including workouts and healthy eating. Whenever I noticed the blob, I would think of my fitness and smile. That's the Spermboy story.

At the time of this writing, it hadn't disappeared, but, boy, have I been to the gym a lot lately! It worked!

Another way to view this story is as a lesson in accepting what you cannot change and determining if you can turn it into something useful. Several years ago, I came across one of my favourite sayings: "When opportunity knocks, make sure you answer, and don't let it get bruised knuckles from banging on your door." I've always taken that a step further, asking, "How can I perceive events, even the challenging ones, not as difficulties, but as opportunities?"

This perspective can open doors that appeared at first to be solid, impenetrable walls. The knowledge that there is value and purpose in everything we experience is a gamechanger. The ability to turn possibilities into realities is certainly a powerful way to transform our lives. I have found throughout my life that imagination can create both inspiration and space for growth in the most unexpected places. Sometimes it might be wise to take a page from your childhood imagination and let a little craziness sneak into your adult life.

Another consideration is developing the self-confidence to act on opportunities that are not quite in your wheelhouse . . . yet.

In the mid-1980s I worked in the investment real estate industry with Harold, my business partner at the time, and my husband and soulmate of the last thirty-four years. As we researched the best way to market and sell our products and services, we discovered that seminars for real estate tax shelters as an investment were the best option. At the time this offered the most effective strategy, so we proceeded to design advertisements for the local newspaper, announcing the date and time of the seminar. The response was exactly as we'd hoped. We sold out a room for 150 people.

The event was in two weeks. We started organizing our informative marketing material that explained the investment opportunity and preparing the sales contracts for our inevitable success. I began the to-do list of event-related tasks and, suddenly, I realized that I was the person who would speak at the presentation. I hadn't done any public speaking at that point. No debates in school, no public speaking experience whatsoever. Never been on a stage. Oops! I realized I had two weeks to learn how to become a public speaker.

Leafing through the Yellow Pages, trying to find public speaking courses, debate courses, anything, I came across a Dale Carnegie course. I phoned the number, and they said they had a class starting the following night. They had weekly sessions, so I would be able to get two classes in before my seminar. I arrived the next evening, eager to start the class that would help me through our sold-out seminar.

What I discovered in those first two sessions were the most powerful messages I could have hoped to hear. I realized that I had several misconceptions about sharing information with an audience. The instructors advised us against writing a speech and memorizing it, which was exactly what I had done. I had already written a draft of my speech and was in the process of memorizing and reciting it, exactly as written. Minutes into the first class, I was learning an entirely new approach and saving myself from a potential public speaking disaster.

The instructors explained that, if we memorized our speeches, we risked reaching a point in the speech where we would forget what came next. If that happened, we would be stuck on stage, unable to continue and debating starting over from the very beginning (not a good choice). The entire speech would be derailed if you didn't know what was coming next. Training solely by memorization all but guaranteed failure.

Rather, they suggested putting each section of the speech into compartments and stories. They told us we could use cue cards and go through the speech as bullet points. We could arrange as we wished, they said, but urged us to learn short stories in short sections. The next session covered animation. They helped us avoid speaking in a monotone voice and encouraged us not to stand still but to move our bodies across the stage.

We did impromptu exercises. For example, they gave us coins to put in our pockets. The instructors told us to pretend that the coins were nails and that we had to put a piece of drywall up on the ceiling. We were to explain our process to the audience as we held the drywall up on the ceiling with one hand and scrambled to get the nail with the other hand. These two lessons and practising in front of the other students as an audience made all the difference in the world. They gave me the confidence I needed to execute a successful presentation. It was amazing to realize that a few evenings spent in a public speaking class could alter the way I connected with people. This little bit of knowledge was all I needed to engage and share with the audience at a whole different level.

The lesson here is that you don't have to be at the peak of your game to try something, or even learn new things. There are countless opportunities at the beginner level. When I walked on stage that night with those 150 people, I picked up a microphone for the first time in my life. I said, "Good evening, ladies and gentlemen, and welcome to our presentation on tax shelters. I'm Gail Taylor."

When the words left my mouth, my voice literally cracked! Had the class covered what to do when that happened? When I heard it, I told myself to carry on. *You've got this, keep going, breathe.* Within the next three sentences, the crack in my voice left and the words flowed out of my mouth. The presentation lasted about an hour and half, and I found myself enjoying the experience and loving that the audience was engaged.

As I neared the end of the presentation, I informed the audience that we would have a question-and-answer session. While I was fielding the questions that came at me from every direction, I realized I loved the spontaneity and fast pace of group Q-and-A sessions. This continued with every future speech I was fortunate enough to deliver; the Q and A is where I excel. This is in part because I make sure I know my material inside out, and in addition because I love being on stage and entertaining an audience.

The seminars turned out to be a great success. Attendees would agree to follow through with one-on-one sessions after the seminars to learn more about the investments. As the business progressed, we were able to sell out most of our projects from seminar marketing alone.

The lesson here is that you can learn things on the fly. There must be a beginning. Whether you start with years of experience or none, the important thing is that you are making that start. The middle and completion are bridges to cross when you come to them. The willingness to begin with no assurance of how and where you will find yourself at a later point is an act of daring, and a wonderful reminder of how it is to feel alive.

Tools for Thought

Developing your self-confidence and your ability to perhaps not take yourself too seriously may require some real effort, but in the Game of Life, it is worth it. It allows you to assess whether jumping in feet first makes sense and perhaps even adds a bit more adventure and excitement to what comes next.

Imagination – Engage It

I feel like our culture might tend to value logic more than imagination, and data more than dreams. There is a downside to this: the wonderful creativity and wild possibilities we often entertain as children can slowly be replaced with a sober understanding of rules, laws, restrictions, and that all-important sense of practicality.

As I discussed imagining my eye floater as a strategy to pay attention to nutrition and exercise, you can use my story as your reminder that you are free to imagine anything and everything in your life. As an adult with bills and schedules and policies, your first instinct may not be to reach for the tool called "imagination," when faced with a challenge.

What if you play a game called "What if?" For example, imagine you have one or more coworkers who are, well, annoying. You might not even have to imagine this because it could be a reality. You pretend (or not) that these well-intentioned people are driving you up the wall with their fondness for gossip, their boring stories, their obsessive focus on insignificant details, and so forth.

Instead of thinking about how draining you find your interactions with them, imagine you are a psychologist or sociologist in an observational study. You can now view them with a detachment that invites many possibilities. The gossipy woman in the sales department—what if as a psychologist you *imagine* that she has been using talking about others to make friends since she was in grade school? She's not trying to run anybody down, she's just lonely. Next time she asks if you have heard about what happened with the fellow in the accounting department, you may realize you aren't annoyed. If anything, you have compassion for this person. You smile, perhaps change the subject, and compliment her on her outfit or new hairstyle.

It is worth noting that this example also helps you to not take other people's behaviour personally. This is a sign of your emotional maturity. Embrace it! Opening your imagination can open many, many avenues for growth.

Self-Confidence – Develop it

If you are a person who lacks self-confidence, don't beat yourself up, because you are not alone. Plenty of people are in the same boat and it might just be a result of some previous experience, perhaps even early in life.

Interestingly, one of the things that contributes to a self-confidence issue can also contribute to developing it to a healthy level. We are again talking about your imagination.

If you let your power of imagination wander into undesirable areas, it can create self-sabotaging scenarios in your mind: *people are laughing at me, insulting me behind my back.* Or maybe it conjures images of you making horrible mistakes at work while everyone is watching. What you imagine can be far from your current reality, or from the result you really want to manifest. If you're not careful, it can leave you feeling diminished and fearful rather than empowered. Or, even worse, you can accidentally turn it into a self-fulfilling prophecy.

You have the choice to train your brain to imagine other things that are not yet part of your reality, and that will allow you to recognize your impressive worth. Here is an example of using your powers of imagination for good: paint in your head a picture of yourself asking for and receiving a raise, giving a presentation, and hearing positive feedback, or whatever you hope to experience. The tool is called creative visualization and Olympic athletes use it all the time. I've been doing it for years, usually while driving by myself or during meditation (often in the bubble bath to combine with a little self-care).

Your powers of imagining the reality you want, one full of growth, excitement, and possibilities, are like muscles. You must use them regularly to keep them in good working order. If you recognize the power of imagination, use it to build up your self-confidence to a healthy level, then, when you are presented with an opportunity, you will be prepared.

Embracing Opportunity

Opportunities are everywhere, and, sometimes, although you realize they are right in front of you, you find throwing yourself into them can pose a challenge. One obstacle you might face is a three-letter word: BUT. You might entertain ideas of taking chances and trying new things, then the word BUT appears, preventing you from embracing the very opportunities that could put you on the path to your best life. This three-letter wet blanket is composed of fear, hesitation, and limiting beliefs, and it can stifle your freedom if you don't challenge it from time to time.

To begin embracing opportunities more frequently, try watching for your "but" and recognizing when it tries to come between you and progress on your journey. It is what you might consider a conditioned response. You may have been taught that caution is better than acting on impulse, and that security is better than risk. Although sometimes that might be true, it is anything but an absolute. You don't want to ignore caution or security; rather, evaluate it, and decide if throwing caution to the wind is in order. This can prevent the "buts" from standing between you and the game-changing experiences you deserve. Try something as simple as replacing "but" with "and."

When I was training myself to embrace opportunities, I was going through a part of my business journey that included significant networking activities. The self-talk had to be trained to push through because it wasn't always second nature for me. I'm an introvert (who just happens not to be shy). When I encountered people that I wanted to meet and talk to, I sometimes decided against it. Why? Here's a bit of my internal dialogue that wasn't serving me (you might recognize it): *"They are probably too busy to chat,* or *what will I have to say that would interest them?"* I worked through this negative talk and shifted to: *"What a wonderful opportunity to introduce myself and meet some like-minded people—this is great!"*

Can you resonate with my story? Or perhaps you heard about events you could have attended to build your skills and expand your horizons, and you didn't attend them because a "but" decided to spoil the fun. *I would love to go, BUT I probably wouldn't fit in/understand/know what to do when I got there."*

Why don't you make the decision to watch out for a tendency to self-sabotage from fear of undesired outcomes, and then shift the internal dialogue to possibilities that can bring new energy and experiences into your life? Embracing opportunities is not a chess game; you do not need to predict what will happen after you try new things. All you need to know is that there is more to gain than you could ever lose when you say yes to the possibilities.

Fake It Till You Make It

With my expanded imagination intact, the "fake it till you make it" concept played an important role in my journey. I used it to help develop my confidence, and to help stop the limiting beliefs from taking control.

Faking it is the opposite of imposter syndrome. It means acting more confident, knowledgeable, or capable than you are (or believe you are). Many of you will do this at some point either in your personal or professional lives—perhaps at a job interview, a first date, or your first time presenting materials to a group. You may give an Oscar-worthy performance, as you are confident the skill you are lacking is something you can develop soon and losing this opportunity isn't something you want to entertain.

While this book is about authenticity being the key to becoming your best self, faking it as a short-term strategy has its merits. When I decided to shift from retirement to keynote speaking, I immediately told myself and everyone I spoke to that I had become a keynote speaker. I worked hard on my internal dialogue strategy to convince my subconscious mind that I had already reached the level I was striving to achieve. My studies convinced me that if you believe you are in possession of something, your subconscious mind will head out on a journey to get it. Ever hear the expression, "Be careful what you wish for . . ."? It fits here. You can use your mantras to achieve this as well. "I am in possession of [*add dream here*]" and I'm loving it!

Imagination, opportunities, and self-confidence are three very different but intertwined parts of who you are and how you play the game of life. I hope you have these areas working at their peak and, if you don't, give yourself a present and develop them further. Let them help you level up your journey through life and CREATE YOUR BEST LIFE!

You and You Alone

Life can be a real challenge. This song inspires you to see all the curveballs as opportunities and realize that you are the only thing standing between you and your goals. It's about taking responsibility. Believe in yourself, and magic happens.

YOU AND YOU ALONE

BY GAIL TAYLOR AND MALLORY BISHOP

I can see you there sitting on the curb
Head in hands, you're trying not to show the hurt
I can hear you whispering your fears straight into the wind
Hoping somebody will hear
but it's only you my dear who can change the story's end

If you could see what I see, the future would look bright
You're beautiful and worthy of everything that's right
You and you alone can choose your destiny
Stand your ground and start to be the change you want to see
Even when you stumble and things seem not okay
you and you alone get to decide if that is where you stay

You might be feeling low, you didn't make the team
It doesn't mean you go and give up, give up on your dreams
Keep looking to the stars and know they're cheering you from home
They never miss a beat, so get up on your feet and dance along the road

If you could see what I see, the future would look bright
You're beautiful and worthy of everything that's right
You and you alone can choose your destiny
Stand your ground and start to be the change you want to see
Even when you stumble and things seem not okay
you and you alone get to decide if that is where you stay

Life gives ups and downs and we can spin out of control
The constant push and pull can really take its toll
Allow the tide to change, 'cause every storm subsides
Your truth is your compass so let it be your guide

If you could see what I see, the future would look bright
You're beautiful and worthy of everything that's right
You and you alone can choose your destiny
Stand your ground and start to be the change you want to see
Even when you stumble and things seem not okay
you and you alone get to decide if that is where you stay
You're enough already

CHAPTER SEVEN

Staying Young

My Story

Age-appropriate behaviour is a concept that humans designed. How you decide what is next in your journey doesn't have to have anything to do with whether you're twenty or thirty or sixty. It has everything to do with how you feel and what you believe is possible. When I decided in my mid-sixties to join the music industry, I realized that many people felt like, once they hit the age of thirty, they were through. They had to completely give up music and move on, in a lot of cases, to an unwanted job that they would be settling for to pay the bills.

Unfortunately, it seems they were listening to the widely accepted business culture focused on finding the next pop star. The entertainment industry is far more than that. There is also talent at every level, including the top, that defies this. Some of my influencers are still active in their eighties, like Paul McCartney, Keith Richards, and Ringo Starr.

In many fields, people happily choose to work beyond the traditional retirement age, and it's often because, to them, working is living. If they follow a purpose or passion as their career, they don't want to retire just because the calendar says it's time.

My story is going to be about attitude, how you address the everyday activities and turn your lemons into lemonade. You have a choice as to how you respond to potential stressors. Remember the concept of "designing your own life" with all the tools I'm sharing? Combine these with what you already know or will pursue in your future learning, and you will be unstoppable!

When life throws its curveballs (big and small) at me, my first thought is: *How can I turn this around and make the best of it*? I had the honour of being friends with Margot Kidder (AKA Lois Lane) for several years. We met when she was contracted as the keynote speaker for the mental health foundation in Edmonton. I, as one of the founders and a current board member, oversaw her travel from the airport and her stay in our city. We had so much in common and bonded instantly. As our friendship grew stronger, she returned to Edmonton to speak as a favour to me, and subsequently invited me to visit her at her home in Montana.

After a wonderful visit, I headed to the airport, and, to my surprise, realized I didn't have a passport. Gone. Lost. The airline informed me I wasn't leaving the country without one and, unfortunately, Montana did not have a Canadian consulate so I would have to fly to Seattle the following day. I called my friend Margot, and, fortunately she was available to host me for another night. When I arrived at the consulate in Seattle, they informed me it would take a minimum of three days to accumulate the documentation required to issue a temporary passport. I had a few major commitments in Edmonton in the following days, so I decided to put my attitude in check and use my internal dialogue and imagination and turn this into a game.

I was now on my own version of *The Amazing Race* and the goal was to get out of Seattle and on a flight back to Edmonton in twenty-four hours—and to have fun with the challenge! Well, it took a village. My executive assistant, my husband, several of my friends, the Seattle passport photo store, and members of my family all played a role. We filled out the mountain of documents, got them notarized, and had documents overnight couriered from Canada. We had friends on standby for calls from the consulate to confirm I was who I said I was, and everything was done at warp speed. The closest I came to a glitch was when the consulate asked a friend what colour my hair was and he responded, "I don't know, I haven't seen her in two years and it's a different colour every time I see her."

The gamechanger here came to me years before when I realized that challenges are just that: challenges. You don't *have* to feel stress if you recognize it as the unnecessary baggage it is. Stress does the opposite of helping you stay young, both mentally and physically.

Another opportunity happened around a travel incident when our connecting flight in Memphis was delayed for four hours. Instead of stressing at the airport, we jumped in a cab and went to Graceland. It's a memory I hold dearly and feel very fortunate to have experienced.

Tools for Thought

Our culture has now decided that there's something called ageism to hold you back, so if you're at a certain age, then your value to a company or to certain situations isn't as significant anymore. THIS IS BUNK! GIVE ME STRENGTH. If someone arbitrarily decided black clothes were inappropriate after the age thirty, would you clean out your closet and throw everything out that was black? Well, it's just as foolish to think you lose value with age.

We go through different phases in life, and, as many societies understand, the elders are considered the wisest and can contribute more valuable insight than others with less experience. As I'm writing this chapter, the 2023 World Happiness Report was just released and, no surprise to me, the happiest people are over the age of fifty. That says it all. Why not learn from others' mistakes instead of repeating them? Modelling is a major peak performance tool.

Attitude

"The longer I live, the more I realize the impact
of attitude on life.

Attitude, to me, is more important than the facts.
It is more important than the past, than
education, than money, than circumstances, than
failures, than successes, than what other people
think or say or do.

It is more important than appearance, giftedness
or skill. It will make or break a company... a
church... a home. The remarkable thing is, we
have a choice every day regarding the attitude we
will embrace for that day. We cannot change our
past.. we cannot change the inevitable. The only
thing we can do is play on the one string we
have, and that is our attitude..

I am convinced that life is 10% what happens to
me and 90% how I react to it.
And so it is with YOU..

We are in charge of our attitudes."

-Anonymous

Attitude makes the difference between getting better and simply getting older. Staying young is about attitude and self-care.

I know you have heard this over and over again, but in case you forgot to FOLLOW THROUGH, here it is again: To become your best self, you must prioritize both your physical and mental well-being. Building a strong foundation means taking care of your body through proper nutrition, sufficient sleep, and regular exercise.

Sleep

Science is still learning about sleep and how vital it is to humans' physical and mental well-being. Before we were able to study the brain in as much detail as we can today, sleep seemed like a period of inactivity, punctuated by dreams and nightmares. In fact, while the body rests, the brain is working through the night, allowing us to awaken the next day with our focus sharp and our outlook bright. Think of the janitors who clean buildings after hours. The office workers come in every morning to see gleaming floors and empty wastebaskets because a crew is dedicated to spending hours preparing for the day ahead.

Brain cell function increases during sleep, as the neurons communicate with each other. Most of us have heard the expression "sleep on it," and scientists are finding that, in fact, cognition occurs during sleep and our brains can work on decision-making and problem-solving while we sleep. We've long thought the body heals and rejuvenates during sleep, and it seems the mind does as well.

Researchers can also attest to sleep's ability to help with memory. It seems our brains perform nightly maintenance on our working memories, essential in helping us to perform daily tasks and retain information. The REM (or rapid eye movement) state of sleep plays a key role in processing memories related to our feelings.

Finally, there is sleep's positive effect on mood. Long before scientists established the link, humans were aware that sleep deficits can make people irritable, anxious, and even depressed. The amount of sleep needed varies from person to person and generally decreases as we age, but sleep is essential to good health. Its effect on mood is a reminder that sleep is something we do for ourselves as much as others. Full disclosure: the tools below are as a result of research and not personal experience. As you will read in a subsequent chapter, my previous sleep challenges revolved around too much sleep versus too little.

If you have trouble sleeping, you've most likely heard this already. The current thinking is that disconnecting from technology has created success for some and allowed them to shift to a good night's sleep. Put down the phone! Or the tablet. Turn off the television, even if you have been using it to lull yourself to sleep. Artificial (blue) light can interfere with your ability to fall and stay asleep. It can block the brain's production of melatonin, a hormone our bodies produce that creates a feeling of drowsiness. Even reading in bed (if it is a good old-fashioned book and not an ebook) is better for the brain (and therefore sleep) than staying stuck to a device. The internet will still be there in the morning! Well, it's worth a try!

A consistent routine is not always possible for everyone, but it seems going to bed around the same time, in a darkened room, is a good beginning for proper sleep hygiene. The twenty or thirty minutes before bed should be spent peacefully. Alcohol, food, and smoking near bedtime are also best avoided.

Insomnia can be caused by brain activity not settling down, which is why many people can't sleep the night before a big trip. Using your imagination and inner dialogue comes in handy once again. Several exercises are available to help you fall and stay asleep. Some people find it helpful to listen to guided imagery of pleasant places or sensations, should counting sheep fail to induce a deep slumber. It's also possible to read about these exercises earlier in the day and perform them at bedtime, should the auditory stimulation prove too strong.

Exercise

Exercising for at least thirty minutes a day not only improves physical fitness but also enhances mental clarity and emotional balance, and might even help you sleep better. Incorporating activities you enjoy into your daily routine has short- and long-term benefits.

Admittedly, some of you might dislike the concept of exercise. This may be because you imagine strange machines in a gym, with uncomfortable clothes and an intimidating atmosphere. THAT'S AN EXCUSE, NOT A REASON! Exercise for fitness can start with a simple twenty-minute walk each day.

Science has shown that exercise helps your bodies as well as your brain. For many people, regular (and high-intensity) exercise is as effective a treatment for depression as prescription antidepressants. People who run, walk, lift weights, or play sports on a daily or even weekly basis can attest to the "natural high" that endorphins create when coursing through the bloodstream.

Think outside the gym if that's not your mojo. I love the energy of the gym, but my husband, who bikes and hikes daily, has no interest in it. We're all different and finding your bliss is the key. Ever tried salsa dancing? It burns calories and it's impossible to resist moving to the music.

Do you like to exercise alone (like Harold)? Put on your headphones and some athletic shoes and you can walk or run as much or as little as you would like, at a time that is convenient for you. Other alternatives are martial arts, gardening, and yoga.

Starting a new exercise program is exciting and requires a degree of self-awareness. If you are new to regular, moderate exercise, pace yourself. Beginners who overdo it risk injury and decide that exercise just doesn't suit them. Your body will thank you if you listen to it when you start reusing long-dormant muscles.

Ask for help. If your efforts at improving your fitness have been underwhelming, trainers and fitness coaches are not just for the wealthy and famous. A few sessions to get started with a trained, qualified professional in your corner might make a major difference.

Time is also worth mentioning here. I have gone through different levels of training and fitness throughout my life and the most intense chapters (training for the NYC marathon and training for a sprint triathlon) turned out to be time boosters. Although I spent more hours training, my energy level and focus increased exponentially, and everything just came together beautifully in the different areas of my life.

Nutrition

Nourishing your body with *wholesome* foods provides the energy and nutrients needed for optimal performance.

Have you ever put low-quality gas in your luxury car? It's possible nothing bad will happen, at least not immediately. Over time, however, you will realize the true cost of habitually putting inferior fuel in your car. It will start knocking. The cheap fuel will damage the engine.

It is the same with the foods you eat. The occasional bag of oily, salty chips will not likely cause a health crisis. However, regular consumption of such food just because it is fast, easy, and packed with calories will take its toll on the body and mind.

Low-quality, ultra-processed food is filler. Lots of calories, plenty of fat, sugar, and salt, but little in the way of the vitamins and minerals needed for physical and mental health. It's not your imagination: regular consumption of ultra-processed foods makes people sluggish. Junk food, especially sugary foods, can cause and worsen depression, according to recent studies.

Fruits and vegetables are your high-test gas equivalent (but you already knew that) and they can be prepared in simple ways and often in minutes. Supermarkets and farmers' markets feature enough locally grown, often organic fruits and vegetables that you can eat a different type every day of the week.

Challenge yourself. Step outside the comfort zone. Are you one of those people that sticks to buying only potatoes, carrots, and familiar but predictable greens? Choose a fruit or vegetable you have never eaten (bonus points if you don't know how to pronounce it), take it home and try it. Millions of people the world over enjoy molokhia and verdolaga. You might, too.

Avoid mindless eating. It's a popular pastime, watching TV or a movie and consuming a generous serving of something loaded with salt, fat, sugar, or all three. By the time we realize what we've done, the entire bag of chips, carton of ice cream, or plate of cookies has somehow disappeared. Consider the advice elsewhere in this book about the value of mindfulness, a kind of awareness. Pay attention to how much, what, and when you eat. The right foods create energy, and energy is used to create your best life.

Staying Young

I loved writing this song and hope it inspires all ages to smile and enjoy the moment. It's never too late to reinvent yourself and go after your dreams. You are in the perfect part of your journey in life at every age. Embrace it!

STAYING YOUNG

BY GAIL TAYLOR AND MALLORY BISHOP

You wonder why I never act my age
Why does my road not line up with my late stage?
I can see you out there searching for the answers
and that truly puts a smile upon my face

Life is full of curves and twists and turns
Seek the best in everything and always heal the burns

Staying young is living for the moment
In this life everybody takes a chance
Staying young means breaking all the boundaries
Staying young is not forgetting why we dance

You ask me where was I at twenty-two
'cause you're worried that your journey's almost through
Honey don't you know your life has just begun
At twenty-two, at thirty-eight, at sixty-one

Life is full of curves and twists and turns
Seek the best in everything and always heal the burns

Staying young is living for the moment
In this life everybody takes a chance
Staying young means breaking all the boundaries
Staying young is not forgetting why we dance

Staying young is living for the moment
In this life everybody takes a chance
Staying young is living for the moment
In this life everybody takes a chance
Staying young means breaking all the boundaries
Staying young is not forgetting why we dance
Staying young is not forgetting why we dance
Staying young is not forgetting why we dance

CHAPTER EIGHT

Time Is on My Side

My Story

Discovering the art of time management marked a seismic shift in my life and I'm sure it can impact yours significantly if you're looking for change. Previously, I found myself trapped in a whirlwind, struggling to keep pace with my Type A personality. My mind was a hub of ideas and ambitions, far surpassing the hours in a day. Guided by the belief that "how you do anything is how you do everything," I became not a perfectionist, but certainly an overachiever.

In my quest for more time, I embarked on a peculiar journey. Convinced that trimming my nightly sleep by a mere two hours could potentially give me an additional month of productivity each year, I ventured into the realm of sleep research. During this period, I stumbled upon a surreal experience that defied all expectations.

I came across an article discussing a local sleep clinic engaged in research on sleeping disorders. Eager to participate, I volunteered for the program and was fortunate enough to be accepted. Subsequently, I underwent an initial consultation with the doctor. This was followed by an overnight sleep session at the clinic, whereby they closely monitored my sleep patterns.

The setting was straight out of a horror movie—I arrived to find a deserted hospital floor cloaked in eerie silence, with faint illumination casting ominous shadows. As I made my way down the hall, the sound of my footsteps reverberated through the empty corridors. Upon reaching the elevator, which was located at the distant end of the building, I realized the elevator was stopped in the basement. Assuming it was the sleep clinic location, I descended. As the doors slid open, I was met with the sight of a nurses' station across the hall. Taking in my surroundings, I observed a peculiar scene unfolding before me. The individuals traversing the area moved with an uncanny resemblance to characters from a poorly scripted zombie flick. It was a surreal moment, one I hadn't anticipated when setting out to find the sleep clinic. Seeking clarification, I approached the desk and was informed that the sleep clinic was on the fourth floor, situated at the far end of the left wing. The staff further elaborated that their clinic was the only other operational unit in the building, serving as a palliative care facility for individuals grappling with muscular disorders.

Back in the elevator and up to the fourth floor, I was starting to think, *Wow, this is a strange adventure.* The left wing required another walk down a long hallway, again with the night lighting and echoes, and, no, I wasn't getting used to it. It was still spooky. I noticed these two big doors at the end of the hallway and realized reaching them was my goal. I arrived, swung open the huge doors, and there was the sleep clinic: brightly lit, well-furnished, and quite inviting, given the circumstances.

I had arrived early, as the doctor had given the sleep clinic staff instructions to make sure that I was the first one they put to bed and the last one they woke in the morning. Within minutes, I was escorted into a small room for the night. It had a single bed with a large medical apparatus next to it. Technicians attached leads (sticky tapes with wires), starting at my head, on my chest, on my sides, and down my legs. Once this procedure was complete, the nurse left the room, shutting the door behind her. There I was, lying still in the dark, alone, and somewhat concerned about rolling over in my sleep.

Suddenly, the nurse's voice came over a speaker. "GAIL, can you hear me?" Once I confirmed her presence, she requested I close my eyes and proceeded with a series of eye-movement instructions. She had me move my eyeballs to the left, move them to the right, up, and, lastly, down. Once we completed this task and she was assured that she could monitor my sleep, she bade me good night and the voice was gone. The next thing I heard was, "GAIL, GAIL, it's time to get up."

Yes, nine hours had passed, and I had slept like a baby. Once unhooked from the machine, I returned to the main area and realized I was the only one there. Everyone else had been discharged earlier and I was now free to go. The information gathered throughout the night was to be sent to the research doctor who would follow up with me in the coming days.

The call came about a week later and off I went to find my miracle solution to add that month onto my life. No such luck. The doctor reported that, after reviewing the reports and analyzing my sleep, his conclusion was that I had an above-average quality night's sleep. Now here is the twist: while he defined my sleep as highly efficient, he informed me that I might reduce my sleep hours by taking antidepressants and said he would prescribe them to me if I was interested. Somewhat shocked, I thanked him and left, knowing that I was not going to entertain that option. I wasn't depressed. I loved life and I was looking for ways to get more time. Taking drugs to achieve this was where I drew the line (this coming from a recovering addict).

In the aftermath of this surreal experience and having tried for two years to find a solution centred around sleep reduction, I knew it was time to take a break and accept the status quo. Today, I wonder, if I had succeeded, would it have been a gamechanger in the wrong direction? Maybe the failure was the success, and the universe had my back. What if a decrease of two hours a night would have resulted in less energy and less focus? Throughout my life I've had many people ask me, "When do you have time to sleep?" to which I giggle and say, "You would be surprised."

I shared this story because it was a bizarre experience and goal that I failed at—and who cares? You win some, you lose some, and life goes on. The win came next, as I moved onto time management as an alternative solution. WOW! Talk about the real gamechanger. I discovered many tools, the first one being Stephen Covey's "Time Management Matrix."

Tools for Thought

Discovering Stephen Covey's four-quadrant method of time management was a revelation that reshaped my life. This system provided a roadmap for determining where to direct my focus and when, offering insights into optimizing both short-term tasks and long-term goals.

At the pinnacle of Stephen Covey's model lie the four quadrants:

Quadrant One: Urgent and Important. Here, tasks demand your immediate attention, and in my case it was mostly because I didn't make them the top priority until they were time sensitive. Working or living in this quadrant can breed stress and can foster a perpetual state of crisis management. This can also result in sacrificing the quality of what you produce, which, in the long run, will reflect unfavourably on you. To mitigate this, and move to Quadrant Two, I devised a strategy of setting deadlines for projects several days ahead of their due dates. This buffer allowed me to handle curveballs or time-sensitive opportunities without succumbing to the chaos of urgency.

Quadrant Two: Not Urgent and Important. Working within this quadrant is truly transformative, as it liberated me from the constraints of time-bound stress, opening avenues for creativity and strategic thinking. Here, if you are anything like me, you will find yourself relaxed, focused, and thoroughly engaged in meaningful endeavours. As mentioned in Quadrant One, this quadrant grants the flexibility to navigate curveballs, like health-related setbacks, without the frantic rush of deadlines looming overhead.

Covey's principles extend beyond professional activities to encompass all facets of your life, as they result in giving you quality time for nurturing your relationships and personal well-being. Activities like socializing with friends, though not urgent, enrich your life immeasurably.

Quadrant Three: Urgent and Not Important. These items are often forms of interruptions concerning other priorities, unfortunately taking up your valuable time. The key for you lies in deciding whether delegation is feasible, or whether you can explain to the person that this isn't a task you are comfortable taking on at this point. While neglecting these tasks entirely may not be prudent, swift processing or delegation ensures they do not hijack your focus from higher-priority pursuits.

Quadrant Four: Not Urgent and Not Important. These are the activities ripe for deletion, such as mindless social media scrolling or excessive gaming. While downtime is essential for recharging, it's crucial to differentiate between meaningful relaxation and aimless time-wasting.

Among Covey's arsenal of tools, prioritizing Quadrant Two proved to be a gamechanger for me. Mastering this quadrant enabled me to live and work in the present, free from unnecessary stress and pressure. Thus, I wholeheartedly advocate making this methodology a cornerstone of your time-management strategy, as it has undeniably transformed my approach to productivity and well-being.

Modifying the above areas to fit my modus operandi and adding a few more brought time management to a non-issue in a short period of time. My nine hour a night sleep became irrelevant as I suddenly felt that time was on my side.

Arrive Early

One tactic you might want to adopt is to arrive fifteen to twenty minutes ahead of scheduled activities, whether business or personal. This buffer allows you to stay on top of your game when you encounter unexpected delays such as heavy traffic or detours, ensuring you remain punctual. Armed with a good book or your walking shoes, you can make efficient use of this extra time while avoiding the stress of tardiness. Over the years this strategy paid dividends in terms of my arriving composed and stress-free, as there were more than a few incidences of time delays.

Prepare for Variations in Others' Timing

Similarly, you can implement a strategy to be ready fifteen to twenty minutes prior to receiving guests or clients, with no time-sensitive tasks scheduled. This allows you to accommodate early arrivals graciously, fostering goodwill and enhancing the overall experience for others. Furthermore, in the office, it provides flexibility in case meetings run over or clients are delayed in arriving, preventing scheduling conflicts and ensuring a smooth flow of engagements.

Have a Backup Plan for Unexpected Downtime

Anticipating the possibility of last-minute cancellations, you can have a backup plan in place to make the most of your unexpected free time. By having this alternative task readily available, you can ensure that every moment remains productive, and rescheduling becomes a non-issue.

Set Realistic Time Estimates

My Achilles' heel was often my tendency to underestimate the time required for tasks. For instance, despite my initial optimism, the timeline for completing this book extended beyond my initial projections. However, by approaching deadlines with flexibility and a commitment to quality, it didn't matter.

You can manage to navigate any challenge without succumbing to undue pressure or stress.

Summary

The above time-management techniques eliminated unnecessary stress from my life and I can't say enough about them. Are you scurrying through your day? Apologizing continuously for being late? Giving up opportunities because there just isn't enough time? If you are, how much stress is associated with your lack of time management and is it worth it?

I keep reminding you that what works for one person may not necessarily work for another; nothing works if you don't implement it, and, yes, it takes time and effort to shift. We all have our own strengths and weaknesses, and the key lies in trying the different tools and strategies and adopting the ones that work best for your individual circumstances.

Time on My Side

This song really is what I went through when I started my previous career as a financial advisor. I LOVED, LOVED, LOVED working in an office and creating investment portfolios, but, boy, can time become a struggle really quickly. If I was not careful, it could have gotten the best of me and zapped some of the fun out of life. I challenge you to grab time by the . . . and take control.

TIME IS ON MY SIDE

BY GAIL TAYLOR AND MALLORY BISHOP

Slap to the snooze again and again
'til I finally make myself roll out of bed
Shower, then coffee to open my eyes
Good lord willing I'll make it on time
Do my hair and makeup, iron my suit
This girl's gotta do what this girl's gotta do
One more cup for the car and I'm on my way
Hoping the traffic won't ruin my day

Doing this dance I don't wanna do
There's gotta be another way to make it on through

Can I break this pattern of rushed and scattered
and learn to enjoy the ride?
If I quit finding fault in all the curveballs
will time be on my side?

Arrive at the workplace with time to spare
Chat with the gang, I'm already prepared
Husband calls "has the dog been fed?"
Did I even kiss him before I left?
Out-of-the-blue calls come in, change the day
making chaos of all I had arranged
Troubled kids, cranky clients all on my plate
All of my early is now running late

Doing this dance I don't wanna do
There's gotta be another way to make it through

Can I break this pattern of rushed and scattered
and learn to enjoy the ride?
If I quit finding fault in all the curveballs
will time be on my side?

So I find my magic, my secret sauce
Now I'm in charge, yeah I'm the boss
Change and challenge go hand and hand
Instead of stumbling now I live to dance

So I make a new pattern that's not rushed or scattered
I'll kick back and enjoy ride
I laugh at it all even those curveballs
'cause time is on my side
Yes time is on my side

CHAPTER NINE

You're My Best Investment

My Story

Throughout my life, I've had a deep yearning for the spotlight. Now, in my late sixties, as I venture into the captivating world of entertainment, I'm excited to be in a peer group with similar traits. It's not unique to me. It's a common thread that weaves through the hearts of musicians, comedians, actors, and anyone else who performs for a crowd. There's a magnetic allure to the stage, a place where many find themselves more at ease than in a room full of people.

Yet, for the longest time, I believed that my longing for attention was somehow wrong. It made me feel like an outsider, within my family and community, and even within my own skin. I struggled to navigate these emotions.

I didn't start out with the self-respect and self-love I have today. We all have different personality profiles and, in my mid-thirties, after completing a training session, I learned there were four major personality types with sixteen sub-types. I discovered I was a Type A, which I personally define as someone who loves being in control, loves being the centre of attention, and craves productivity. Wikipedia describes it as *an individual that is outgoing, ambitious, rigidly organized, highly status-conscious, impatient, anxious, proactive, and concerned with time management*—well, if the shoe fits. . . . These traits turned out to have some great benefits for me, but I had some serious issues with them when I was a young person. I took self-sabotage and hurting my loved ones to a whole new level.

When I was fifteen, I decided to hitchhike across Canada with my boyfriend, in the middle of winter, with seven dollars in my pocket. Yes, you read that right. Remember, I was spiralling and not too swift. We mostly slept in barns and gas station bathrooms and received food stamps and meals from churches that we approached. When we reached Revelstoke, a beautiful town in the Rocky Mountains in British Columbia, we were involved in a car accident with our ride.

I was taken into custody by the police for running away from home as a minor. They contacted my mother and had her send train fare to transport me back to Ottawa. In the meantime, they moved me to a group home for wayward girls, where I was to remain for a number of days until the train ride could be arranged.

That experience turned out to be one I will never forget. I might have been honing my skills as a performer even then, because, apparently, I came off as a responsible young lady to the couple running the group home. They asked if I would babysit their two small children so they could have a night out. I agreed and, shortly after they departed, the five other teenage foster girls staying at the house decided I deserved a beating. They circled me and threatened to beat me to a pulp because I obviously thought I was better than them. With a bit of luck and the gift of the gab, I was able to talk them out of it by offering them cigarettes and joints that I explained I would be able to get from my boyfriend the following day.

How I was going to pull that off was beyond me, but, hey, it kept my ribs intact for the night.

I shared that whole runaway story because, had I not been so insecure within my own family structure, I'm not sure I would have bolted. It might have been a few years down the road before I learned anything from this high-risk adventure, but, eventually, I realized facing conflict head on is a better solution than running.

If you can develop a stronger level of self-awareness, you can use personal-growth tools to reach higher levels. I blamed my family for my insecurity and, with such a low level of emotional maturity, I wasn't able to understand their reality and how much pain and stress and worry they would have to experience because of my actions.

I am fairly certain it was at this point that my mother arranged for my future counselling. The gentleman with whom I worked was a godsend. He actually remained in my life as a therapist off and on for about eighteen years, until I moved to Edmonton in 1990.

It wasn't until several years after my hitchhiking adventure that I started on my journey of studying personal growth and peak performance. Reflecting back helped me understand just how dysfunctional and unaware of others' emotions I was. Picture my mother's situation. First, she lost her husband, and in the quest to raise her six children the best she could, I decided to run away and add more emotional turmoil to her life. If I could talk to my fifteen-year-old self I'd say, "What a jerk move that was."

Working with the counsellor, I discovered that I wasn't actually broken and that self-love wasn't selfish. I did, however, have some major work to do to get out of my head. How can you be proud of yourself when pride is one of the Seven Deadly Sins? Was it really OK to be different, to want attention, to crave productivity, and to take pride in your achievements? Was I becoming strong, confident, and successful or was I becoming vain, selfish, and greedy? These were questions for which I struggled to find answers. Being able to navigate through some of the deep-rooted beliefs of my past was pretty healing and came in handy years later when I started to design my own life.

Fast forward to my thirties. I continued to improve in creating my best life on a daily basis. Things were quite different from my early years of turmoil and uncertainty. I liked myself and although I was still making mistakes, I was confident that I was doing my best and that I would continue to progress with time.

My growing awareness of the people around me was a gamechanger, a welcome development for me, as well as everyone else in my life. I was able to create a network with mentors, friends, and amazing clients. Working with and for them was an honour.

There were several areas that were instrumental in my shift. Embracing these values and living a life that incorporated them fully allowed me to begin living my best life.

Tools for Thought

We discussed limiting beliefs and the influence of self-talk in an earlier chapter, The Game of Life, highlighting how important these are in shaping our view of ourselves and the world around us. What we tell ourselves matters, and this includes the commitments we make to ourselves.

For some of you, it is easy to dismiss keeping your word to yourself. No one else will know, so what is the harm? The harm is to you. You harm yourself when you don't honour your commitments. Self-harm is harm that doesn't belong in your best life.

Self-harm is the opposite of self-care, which is the goal.

Integrity

Do you have a personal code of ethics? We are not talking about laws, but values. Have you ever asked yourself if there are things you would never do under any circumstances? Are there actions you would consider permissible in some situations? Your ideas about right and wrong, about absolutes and situational ethics, give insight into how you develop a sense of integrity. It is a valued commodity, although it is not for sale.

Demands for integrity are everywhere. Job descriptions specify the candidate must have integrity. People on internet dating sites specify that they are looking for someone with integrity. We tend to think of integrity as something like honesty; a person with high integrity is principled.

Integrity has another meaning, and it is often used when describing things rather than people. It means united, complete, or whole. It may help to understand personal integrity as similar to structural integrity.

People with integrity have a sense of how the whole picture of relationships looks. They are aware how much they give and how much they take, and aim for a balance. They respect others and expect respect in return. People with integrity maintain their own boundaries and understand that others do the same, although possibly with different boundaries.

As for the Golden Rule (treating others as we would like to be treated) versus the Platinum Rule (treating others as they wish to be treated), people with high integrity can manage to do either without behaving in ways contrary to their personal code of ethics.

It may not be your primary goal, but if you have high integrity, you earn the respect of others because you are true to yourself. There is a steadiness to a person with high integrity; wins and losses are handled with equanimity; the core of who you are remains the same, never mind the score.

When you live with integrity, you are aware of your values and you're not riddled with conflict from trying to be what you are not. Rather than wearing a different face with every person you meet in an attempt to gain favour and manipulate others, integrity compels you to be truthful about who you are—to others and especially to yourself.

I've had my integrity tested many times through the years as I'm sure you have. Sometimes your most challenging tests are between you and yourself—or the term I use affectionately: me, myself, and I.

The true measure of our character arises when we are faced with challenging circumstances, where integrity becomes an internal dialogue with oneself. I recall a particular instance where a client approached me, seeking a summer job for their daughter, who was exploring a career in finance. Despite my financial constraints, the client graciously offered her services as an unpaid intern. I accepted, expressing gratitude. From the onset, I committed myself to tracking her hours diligently, with a promise to compensate her fairly once my practice flourished. Over the years, I kept this commitment alive, a quiet pact hidden in my to-do list. Several years later, when I finally had the means, I fulfilled my promise. I did, however, experience some internal dialogue justifying both options. The young woman and her family had moved on, grateful for the experience, with no expectation of remuneration. Yet, for me, it was about upholding the standard of integrity I'd set for myself, investing in my own character.

Honesty

Telling the truth should not be complicated, but sometimes you find speaking your truth can hurt people's feelings, and you may struggle as to where to draw the line.

Human communication is influenced by tone, body language, and each receiver's unique perspective. General George S. Patton said, "Say what you mean, and mean what you say." Although the origin of the addendum to this is uncertain, some people finish the aphorism with: "And don't say it mean."

The question often becomes: is it worse to hurt someone's feelings than it is to be dishonest, especially if it's a little white lie? This depends on the role honesty plays in your life or the circumstance. Many spouses would not consider telling their partners that they don't like the new haircut. Let's look at honesty in the bigger picture. I'm suggesting being honest with your words and not lying to impress someone or to make things easier on you because perhaps they won't approve of what you did. This value is amazing and removes a lot of stress associated with "What if they find out?" When I was in active addiction, I told my share of lies and often for no significant reason. It just seemed easier and, as I travelled down the road of personal growth and designing my own life, the shift was another gamechanger. Wherever you are in your journey, consider the benefit of honesty. It's powerful.

Consistency

Ideally, your actions and words match, which elevates your well-being and your reputation. Aiming for consistency in your life is a mark of maturity. Sometimes you learn this after spending time on the receiving end of another person's inconsistency. Consistency benefits both the giver and receiver. Consistency shows that you are trustworthy and reliable, qualities that cement the relationships you need in many areas of your life: business, family, friends, and community allies.

Overcoming Self-Sabotage and Insecurity

Self-sabotage is often the result of fear. Feeling uneasy about success may sound counterintuitive, but humans, like other animals, are wary of the unknown. Especially for people who succumb to limiting beliefs and consider themselves "not worthy" in some way. Fear may be the first and most powerful response to the possibility of attaining new opportunities.

If you believe that success is undeserved, it can cause you to behave in a self-sabotaging way. Rather than wait for the failure that seems inevitable, a self-sabotaging person hastens the fall from greatness. You might say or do things to harm your work, alienate others, or withdraw into yourself rather than enjoy the success that is rightfully yours.

Insecurity is a kind of parasite, feeding off limiting beliefs about worth, competence, and potential. A few qualities we've discussed earlier are antidotes to insecurity: honesty and self-awareness. If you have those you can acknowledge and appreciate your positive qualities, your accomplishments, and your potential for limitless greatness.

Understanding Your Built-in Personality Style

Making the most of your personality style is simply the logical extension of one of the key messages of this book: be true to yourself, because yourself is pretty fantastic! To better understand our complex personality styles, it may be useful to use an example from the animal kingdom. There are some 200 breeds of dogs recognized by the AKC, not counting the untold number of mixed breeds.

Like people, they come in many shapes and sizes. They also have different temperaments. Dogs bred for herding large animals, for example, have incredible stamina and energy. Other breeds are geared more toward guarding. They are watchful, protective, and not easily intimidated.

It's possible to draw a parallel with people. Some people are like basset hounds: they seldom rush, they don't get overly excited very often, and they are great to have around. Other people are like border collies: they hate to sit still, are easily bored, and enjoy a challenge.

People who love activity and excitement can make themselves (and the people around them) miserable when they try to be what they are not: sedate and calm. The world needs all kinds of people. We all have something to offer just by being our authentic, unapologetic selves. In the recommended reading section of this book you'll find further information of personality types if you are interested in understanding yourself further.

You're My Best Investment

This song was inspired after many years of self-reflection that resulted in my finding myself. Trusting in my ability to be true to myself and those around me gave me the strength and confidence I needed to quit with the self sabotaging. Hope you decide to do the same!

YOU'RE MY BEST INVESTMENT

BY GAIL TAYLOR AND MALLORY BISHOP

Thank you for supporting me
when no one else was there
I know at times how hard it was
It seemed I didn't care
I took most things for granted
that should have mattered more
Yet you hung in and helped me grow
to someone who's assured

I treated others kinder
and I gave them more than you
I did that cause it seemed right
what I was "supposed" to
I knew deep down you needed me
yet I didn't make the time
But looking back I know now
you've been in every rhyme

I'm ready now to love you
Better late than never
We still have work to do
I think we will forever

No more broken promises
or putting you aside
You've got my full attention
and you deserve my time
I'll release my fear and let go of resentment
'cause I finally realized
you're my best investment

I'm fully committed to the new patterns I'll make
I know it won't be easy
and some habits need to break
The past does not define me
and it will show me where to change
I'll learn as I go along
and I know you'll keep the faith

I'm ready now to love you
Better late than never
We still have work to do
I think we will forever

No more broken promises
or putting you aside
You've got my full attention
and you deserve my time
I'll release my fear and let go of resentment
'cause I finally realized
you're my best investment

Self-love isn't selfish and I finally understand
I can be my own best friend
and hold onto my own hand
I may not be perfect
and it may take me a while
but when I see you in the mirror
from now on I will smile

I'm ready now to love you
Better late than never
We still have work to do
I think we will forever

No more broken promises
or putting you aside
You've got my full attention
and you deserve my time
I'll release my fear and let go of resentment
'cause I finally realized
you're my best investment
I finally realized
you're my best investment

PART THREE

CURVEBALLS—INSIDE AND OUT

There were a few of my life's curveballs that resulted in decades of emotional turmoil for me and my family. I'm lucky to be coming from a place of healed scars and not open wounds as I share these stories in more detail.

CHAPTER TEN

Wings

My Story

I have a soft spot for people whose loved ones are in active addiction. It's a disease that doesn't just affect the addict; it affects everyone close to the addict and even those not so close, like coworkers, or perhaps someone indirectly affected that hasn't even met the addict.

In my experience, people suffer greatly when the addict is a family member.

This story is mine and my son's. I have his permission to share it with you. I've told it many times, to individuals and large audiences, in both personal and professional settings. Interestingly, people who have loved ones dealing with other serious illnesses have told me that handling those challenges requires similar tools.

Because I can only speak from experience, this is a story about addiction specifically. However, the broader message is about understanding and navigating a parallel journey with someone who is struggling. Traumatic as this experience can be, it is still possible for you to find happiness on this journey. You can be productive and centred. You can learn to manage stress when it threatens the stability necessary to withstand the uncertainty inherent in addiction.

I know you can experience these positive feelings. Again, I speak from experience. With a commitment to healthy boundaries and the tools to practise self-care, you can prevent a loved one's journey from overtaking your centredness.

My journey began with my relentless pursuit of success, fueled by ambition and passion. Amidst the frenzy of socializing and work, I failed to realize that my son was not receiving the attention he needed from me. As I have mentioned elsewhere in the book, my early life was marked by loss, trauma, and addiction. I have also discussed the moment when the light of understanding fell upon me, and I realized the path along which I was travelling was a dead end. Over the years, I studied many approaches to happiness and fulfillment and developed one that worked for me. What I have not shared with you until this point is the timing of these events.

When I first became interested in personal growth and peak performance, I was still in denial about my own substance abuse. As addicts often do, I had ways of rationalizing my behaviour. I just enjoyed partying, I told myself. It was not as if I was unconscious in an alley. It was the early 1980s and the theme of the era was work hard, play hard . . . so I did. In my professional life, I was familiarizing myself with the tools for success. As far as my personal development, I didn't truly comprehend that I was an addict. It is worth mentioning that, forty years ago, knowledge of addiction was not part of the mainstream as it is today. I remember my first prenatal appointment, telling my doctor that I smoked cigarettes and marijuana. His recommendation was to limit consumption to ten a day of either one.

For me, it seemed very simple: I knew I loved to party and did it as much as possible. I did not understand that my nonstop lifestyle was dysfunctional. What I am certain of now is that I was a workaholic, determined to party every night with mind-altering substances. I believed that, as long as my son was with good caregivers and I had some quality (versus quantity) time with him, then our lives would be wonderful. I was mistaken.

In retrospect, the situation went from bad to worse when my son turned twelve. The two of us moved across the country, I left his father, brought a new man into his life, and put him in a new school. These were echoes of my own troubling experiences when I was twelve. It may not come as a surprise to readers that my son began experimenting with drugs and quickly became dysfunctional. And, yes, I was still partying.

As he grew more and more rebellious, his life quickly spiralled downward. Those readers who have experienced similar situations have a pretty good idea of what came next: my son's life became one of group homes, contracts with social services, and jail time. My attempts to help him were met with anger, as he blamed me and the mistakes I'd made for his addiction and troubled life. He hated me with an intensity that frightened me.

I remember how confrontational and verbally abusive his phone calls would be when I refused to give him money. For readers unfamiliar with the games addicts play, an addict does not phone and ask for money for drugs. They claim they need the money to pay the electric bill or the phone bill or to pay rent, so they don't get evicted.

While my own substance use was not as intense as my son's, I stopped using mind-altering substances daily for the first time while my son was an active addict. Helping him through this became a new priority, which had its own issues, as I quickly had to learn what I could control and what I couldn't.

Whether it was drugs or alcohol, somehow I had plateaued at an early enough stage of the disease at which I was still considered functional. When I went to a family day at my son's rehabilitation centre, I asked the counsellor about my situation. Why didn't I need a rehab centre to stop drinking and using drugs? He informed me I had experienced what they called "hitting a high bottom." Hitting bottom is a term used to describe being in such a low place that addicts start to see things for what they are. It's when the pain of staying the same is stronger than the pain of seeking change.

For an addict, it could be a legal issue, like receiving a DUI or an event on the domestic front, such as having your spouse and children leave. It is different for everyone. For me, it was when I realized my son needed my help in more ways than I had been offering.

Eventually, my son became addicted to opioids, and we grew estranged for a few years. I share this story today as he is in recovery, and we have now become best friends. We built a new relationship with one another as two adults who'd weathered the storms of addiction and emerged from them stronger and more compassionate. Learning to love my son in a healthy way while he was in active addiction was another gamechanger and the key to maintaining my own happiness.

I am also pleased to say that I am coming from a place of healed scars, not open wounds. The road was filled with obstacles, but, together, we learned to navigate the challenges, letting go of resentment and regrets. I learned what was in my control and realized that love alone could not heal an addict; it required patience, understanding, and a genuine knowledge of what codependency, enabling, and boundaries truly meant. For me, it was about being there for him when he was ready to get clean and without letting the high drama consume me.

The process was not easy, by any means. I spent countless hours studying the disease, in therapy and practising self-care to determine what I could change (my behaviour and responses) and what I could not (other people, especially the addict). I definitely had to learn how to let go and engage in activities that nurtured my own growth and well-being. As I became adept at using tools, I allowed myself to enjoy life, free of guilt.

Both my son and I were also fortunate that one of my sisters, a beautiful soul, helped with his journey to shift from street opioids to methadone, a controlled substance that's part of a harm-reduction program offered by the medical community.

I am so lucky that he embraced sobriety when he did. Drugs have become an epidemic in today's world. If he were an active addict today, I do not know if I would still have a son. Drugs have only grown more powerful and can end lives in seconds. Substance abuse is deadlier than ever.

My son shared a story that centred around young, middle-class drug users. They want to party with mitigated risk and in these cases, they prefer pharmaceuticals. They go to parties and take prescription opioid pills to get high. The illegal drug manufacturers realized this and using fentanyl and carfentanil as cutting agents they started to make their own pills to mimic the look of mainstream pharmaceuticals. They are essentially exact replicas of the prescription drug, stamp and all, leaving the users unaware of what's counterfeit and dangerous.

Many places around the world, including Canada and the United States, are experiencing higher levels of addiction than ever before. The opioid epidemic has mushroomed and is terrifying.

At the time of writing this book, there were twenty-two overdose deaths each day in Canada and over 100 daily in the United States. In 2016, Canada reported just over 2,800 deaths from opioid overdoses. In 2022, the number was staggering at more than 7,300. Many cities are dealing with increasing rates of addiction and homelessness.

In April of 2016, the Canadian government declared the opioid crisis a national health emergency. Millions of dollars in aid have helped fund programs devoted to education, rehabilitation, and prevention of opioid abuse. Despite nearly a decade of government and private organizations' efforts, the numbers are troubling. In the United States, a parallel story is unfolding with no end in sight.

Tools for Thought

If the gamechangers we have discussed in this chapter are part of your reality, or you have a parallel journey with another dysfunctional relationship, here are tools to study and use. They can help you to incorporate self-care, contentment, and healthy limits into your life. To help you create real change and give you your power back—KEEP READING. For those not living with these scenarios, I'm hoping this information will give you some insight and help you understand the inner workings of these challenging relationships, particularly in the world of addiction.

If you know my story, the reason I have a soft spot for all the loved ones of addicts becomes obvious. I would like to spend the rest of this chapter discussing the options available to help others stay healthy, happy, and productive. Some of my findings will help you and others won't be a fit. Choose what helps you in your situation.

Being Your Own Advocate

I listened to my intuition—or "gut feelings," as some people call them—when assessing the people I invited into my life to help me. I am thankful I trusted my gut when I experienced a misalignment with a therapist. I explained my situation to a new psychologist, sharing that, for the most part, my life was going great; my job was wonderful, my husband was wonderful, and so on. However, I was needing additional coping strategies to deal with the challenge of having a child in active addiction and living a high-risk lifestyle.

She told me to tell my son that he was dead to me and that I didn't want anything to do with him until he was clean. Only then would he be allowed to get in touch with me. She expanded on this by saying if I didn't do what she was suggesting, he would take me down; it was just a matter of time.

I had to move on to another therapist. I can't speak for others on this approach, but it wasn't one I was comfortable with, nor one I would consider implementing. I wanted my son to always know that, if he was hitting bottom and wanted help to enter rehab, I would be his advocate to help make it happen. That was the point of therapy and self-care: to stay strong.

The phrase "tough love" is often used to describe the approach I needed in order to deal with my scenario and my son being an active addict. I absolutely believe in having boundaries, but not the kind this therapist suggested. My values demanded that I create a healthy distance with my son, not erect a wall between us to last a lifetime.

Her strategy and choice of words were incompatible with my beliefs and the direction I thought was helpful. I'm sharing this story because if you have tried group therapy or an individual therapist and it didn't resonate with you, don't give up; continue to search for the right fit. I've heard too many people give up too soon, painting therapy or support groups with a broad brush, thinking it doesn't work for them because they tried it once. There are different approaches and only through trial and error will you find the ideas and practices that work for you.

People involved in addiction and recovery have developed an extensive vocabulary of terms to define behaviours, feelings, techniques, and concepts. These can help us understand what we are experiencing as well as provide us with options to navigate the landscape more easily and develop the tools we need. Remember, this isn't a one-and-done fix, and it will require ongoing maintenance, open-mindedness, and a willingness to continue to grow and heal.

Boundaries

What comes to mind upon hearing the word "boundary"? Electric fences? Unscalable walls? When we talk about relationships and addiction, boundaries are healthy and necessary, but not necessarily physical in form. What is also important to remember is that addicts may tend to dislike boundaries and attempt to push against another's efforts to set limits.

Boundaries are rules and guidelines that you establish to protect yourself, people close to you, and the addicted person. They ensure that you are not taken advantage of or abused by your loved one.

Setting limits sounds like something parents do with willful toddlers . . . or teens. At first, it can be stressful and exhausting. In truth, setting boundaries with coworkers, family members, and friends is part of loving ourselves. It may not be easy or pleasant to begin enforcing boundaries with addicts, but, eventually, you will be glad you did.

An example of setting a healthy boundary for me was letting my son know I would no longer take his phone calls unless those calls were requests for help in attaining treatment. Calls for money, material goods, a place to crash, a sympathetic ear, or a ride to the dealer's house would no longer be available. I mentioned above that this was necessary for me because of my son's anger toward me.

I have witnessed other situations in which the addict was not angry or aggressive in any way and their parents were able to set different boundaries. They could take the calls, encourage recovery, and remain an active part of their loved one's life. Every situation is different.

It's important to understand that addiction is powerful and that it can take several attempts, even in rehabilitation centres, for someone to establish long-term recovery.

Control (or Not)

Understanding what is in your control and what isn't becomes very important at this juncture. I remember helping my son into rehab, followed by setting him up in an apartment with furniture and a few months' rent, only to have him relapse and lose it all within six months. I accepted this as a possible outcome from the beginning, because it was out of my control. Wanting to set conditions is understandable, but it is impossible to control the outcome. Relapse is considered a symptom of the disease and it is part of what can create an emotional roller coaster. If you allow yourself to believe your actions of support and help somehow would control the outcome, you're mistaken. There is a personal-growth/peak-performance tool I'll mention here: don't take it personally. Remember you're on a parallel journey and you only get to do you.

Sometimes it takes some real sacrifice and self-awareness to create your intertwined or estranged story. The story I just shared regarding the apartment involved another dimension that involved my work. At the time, I worked as a financial advisor, managing retirement portfolios. I was in a highly trusted role with many regulations.

I approached my manager and subsequently our legal team with this scenario: I was setting my son up in an apartment straight out of a rehabilitation centre for a drug addiction. I wanted to co-sign on the lease; however, I would not be paying the rent if he relapsed and started living a lifestyle in active addiction. My strategy was to wait until the landlord evicted him and then pay the outstanding back rent and settle the account. This could have involved some level of outstanding charge against me during the process, which I needed to confirm would not affect my employment.

They assured me that this was no more serious than a jaywalking ticket and I would be in the clear. They all wished me well and hoped for my family's success going forward. Unfortunately, it didn't work. This wasn't the turning point for my son. However, I truly believe recovery can involve a dance of three steps forward and two back. He has subsequently shared that the tools he picked up during this segment of his journey were part of his toolbox in recovery, still being used today.

As you can see, setting boundaries is somewhat abstract and different for everyone and changes during the journey. For me, spending thousands of dollars on rehabilitation programs that may or may not work was a no-brainer. I did it every chance I got. Spending thousands of dollars supporting the active addiction lifestyle was what I worked hard at avoiding, which brings us to our next term: enabling.

Enabling

Enabling is defined as the process by which a person contributes to the self-destructive or compulsive behaviour of another person. Instead of helping someone who is struggling with addiction, an enabler may find themselves inadvertently promoting or permitting their loved one's continued substance misuse.

While I cannot list them all, here are some enabling behaviours that may allow addicts to escape the consequences of their behaviour: performing household chores the addict is capable of doing, providing money and transportation for the addict, bailing the addict out of jail, and lying to employers or other authorities to keep the addict out of trouble. I have been an enabler and I have also been in a relationship with an addict whereby I was no longer an enabler.

A turning point for me was learning that enabling was harmful to the addict and helped the disease take hold and remain active. That knowledge allowed me to shift to a healthier place. Enabling my son *did* serve a purpose for me, by alleviating the guilt I felt for my role in his challenges. My thought process centred around the belief that, if I had been a better mother and not struggled with my own substance abuse, my son wouldn't have been in this situation. It's a version of guilt I have heard many parents articulate, even the ones that never missed a beat like I had. Their common thought seemed to be: *What could I have done differently to have prevented this?*

Often, the answer is nothing. Regardless, we cannot change the past. We can use our self-awareness and emotional maturity to take inventory of the past and use it in productive ways going forward. If you are playing a part with enabling behaviour, chances are you have some experience with our next term: codependency, and the emotional roller-coaster ride that comes with this one.

Codependency

Words and phrases that describe codependency have crept into the English language in recent years. Sometimes when we talk about a person who "needs to be needed," or someone who has "the disease to please," or the more common "people pleaser," we are talking about a mild form of codependency. Substance abuse can introduce a new level of codependency. I think when it comes to having a loved one in addiction, all bets are off.

Psychology Today defines codependency as, "a term used to describe a relationship in which, by being caring, highly functional, and helpful, one is said to support, perpetuate, or enable a loved one's irresponsible or destructive behavior." When we refer to a codependent relationship between a person and an addict, the results can be tragic. If an active addict has a relationship with a person (or people) who encourage rather than discourage addictive behaviour (often not realizing that is what they are doing), dysfunction reigns. The relationship can become a vicious cycle of an addict abusing a substance, and the codependent cleaning up the mess the addict leaves behind in an effort to feel valued for their caretaking.

I spent a number of years as a codependent, enabling my son's early years of addiction because I didn't know any better. Even once I understood, it still took time to shift my thinking. I've played the mind game of, "if I don't visit him in jail and give him money he'll become a criminal," or "if I don't pick him up and drive him to his dealer's he might steal a car." I was literally living on the emotional edge whereby any time the phone rang, my heart skipped a beat. *Is he dead? Is he in trouble?* I managed these feelings with professional help. Working with psychologists, reading and studying books, attending support groups, and developing a realistic plan designed for me that I could follow changed the way I processed the situation. This brings us to self-care.

Self-care

First, it is important to clarify what self-care is *not*. It is not selfish or frivolous behaviour. Engaging in it is not proof that you do not care about the addict in your life. Self-care does not harm the addict or deprive the addict in any way.

Sometimes when people travel on airplanes, they are surprised to learn that adults should put oxygen masks on themselves before putting them on children. It would seem that the child's welfare should come first. This emergency drill on airplanes is actually a reminder that children need the adults around them to function at full capacity, especially in a crisis.

The same principle applies when helping someone onto the path of sobriety. The demands of enforcing boundaries while offering support require our mental and physical strength. Keep the reservoirs full with daily acts of kindness . . . toward yourself.

While it may sound like a fancy New Age term, self-care is based on practices that are centuries old. The concept of mindfulness, with its emphasis on awareness of one's breathing and focus on the present moments, has roots in Buddhism. It is an activity that costs nothing, can be performed at any place and time, and keeps racing thoughts and regrets from overwhelming us.

Other examples of self-care may be more familiar, but are no less critical to maintaining vitality. Avoiding highly processed food, and getting regular exercise and rest all reduce stress levels, keeping health issues at bay.

Emotional stress of any kind can absolutely result in physical ailments. I've seen first-hand how being in a codependent relationship with an active addict and the emotional drama that comes with that can feel like stress on steroids. Headaches and backaches are common when people spend their days with their muscles tensed, fearing a call about the addict from the jail or the hospital, or worse. Thoughts of what the addict is doing or failing to do can leave a family member's stomach in knots.

Sharing the journey through life with an addict can also harm a person's mental health. While mental illness isn't contagious the way viruses are, it is part of the human experience to sympathize and empathize with loved ones. People may become depressed, blaming themselves for another person's addiction. If they feel guilty, people can punish themselves in ways that harm their mental and physical well-being.

Self-care is all about shifting the control from the external activities being thrown at you to an internal mindset and lifestyle design that give you back your power, emotionally and physically. Remember the chapter "Staying Young"? It's amazing how healing taking care of yourself can be.

Compartmentalizing

Compartmentalization is a stress-management tool that I use to deal with situations and feelings that threaten to overwhelm me and have negative effects in other areas of my life. Unlike the unhealthy response of denial, which involves pretending the addict and their behaviour do not exist, compartmentalization allows you to put the situation in a psychological space that contains the stress and uncertainty of loving and living with an addict.

After I met with the therapist who insisted I cut off all contact with my son, I felt she must not have realized I was using compartmentalization as a tool. I could work, play, and deal with all other areas of life without focusing on or stressing over my son's challenges until I was ready to address them. I would pick the right time of day for me and deal with whatever was on the table.

Community Participation and Resources

Many people I have talked to over the years have shared feelings of hopelessness and a sense that they had nowhere to turn for help. One reason is the stigma that still exists around mental disorders and addiction, despite the availability of scientific information about these conditions. Let's define stigma: a misconception that their drug use and related behaviours are a choice, rather than a compulsion, and that they are to blame for their medical condition. Studies show that terms like "junkie" can feed negative biases and dehumanize people.

A common response to being judged or feeling ashamed is to keep the situation a secret. You might try to justify your secrecy with the excuse, "no one will understand." Unfortunately, secrets come with a price. The phrase "You're only as sick as your secrets" exists for a reason. Secrets can create self-loathing, negative talk, anxiety, and stress around being outed.

It's a powerful move to break the silence and shatter the secrecy, rather than let it fester within you and undermine your self-esteem. Once your secret is no longer a secret, it loses its power. You regain control and the ability to work on self-care. I am not suggesting that you shout it from the rooftops or write a tell-all book about your struggles (leave that to me). However, a therapist, support group or well-trusted friend or family member fit in here nicely.

For many years I was somewhat private as I went through my struggles. I'm sure there are a few people reading this book that knew me for years and were unaware of what I was going through; there were many others that understood the situation completely.

I found over the years when I shared my story one on one with a colleague or client, the response was often very similar. "My sister's son is in the same situation." "I have a nephew that's an addict and my brother is beside himself." "My daughter is struggling with addiction, but nobody knows." This reaction of, "I know someone going through the same thing," or "I'm going through the same thing," is all too common.

In addition to giving you some clarity on the current community landscape with respect to our opioid epidemic, I hope this section gives you inspiration and understanding that you are not alone and there is help and support for you. Taking this a step further, I hope you take the initiative to design your best life and incorporate the boundaries, change enabling and codependency behaviour, and compartmentalize when needed. Above all, take the time for self-care.

Naloxone - A Story that Opened my Heart

I attended a fundraising breakfast organized by a mental health foundation in early 2023. I was absolutely amazed and proud of what happened following the event. It was largely attended by the business community: lawyers, accountants, financial advisors, bankers, and entrepreneurs. After the keynote speaker, Johann Hari, completed his presentation on addiction, a local health-care provider took to the podium to make an announcement. She explained that there was a table set up near the exit and they would be handing out free naloxone kits (also referred to as Narcan). She explained that if, when you are out and about and saw someone overdosing (which, unfortunately, wasn't uncommon in the downtown core of our city and perhaps yours), you could save their life by following the steps explained in the kit.

Naloxone rapidly reverses the life-threatening effects of an opioid overdose. It is often used by first responders but can easily be administered by laypeople, family members or friends. She also explained that it was harmless if you accidentally injected someone that wasn't overdosing. She made a joke about someday shocking her audience by stabbing herself in the leg with the needle to show no harm would come to her.

Here is the part of the story that amazed me. There weren't enough supplies for the long line of people, most of them white-collar types, waiting to get a kit! Think about what I just described: a community of professionals lined up to get a kit that they could carry in their briefcases or purses in the event they would have the opportunity to save a life, and not just any life, that of an addict. My eyes are watering as I recall this amazing testament of compassionate human nature.

Resources and ideas to move forward

If you are considering being the advocate when the time is right, research the treatment centres in your area and be prepared. Find out costs, waiting lists, intake requirements, and any other information that will help you when the window opens.

1. To find group support in Canada or the United States, you can call Al-Anon at 888-425-2666 or Nar-Anon at 800-477-6291.
2. Research and read a few books on addiction. There is a wide variety of approaches, from understanding the medical/science around addiction to learning coping mechanisms. There is no right approach. You'll know what information will help you with your situation.
3. As the advocate, if you choose that route, it might help to know what second-stage housing is available after the rehabilitation process.
4. Research self-care programs. I personally found that taking the time to watch videos (TED Talks are great), read articles, and actually design a personal self-care program works. You could start with something very simple, such as: Monday, I will go to a support group meeting. On Tuesday, I will spend thirty minutes reading or watching a video on addiction and how it affects the family. Wednesday, I will go for a long walk, meditate, or take a bubble bath. Thursday, I will look into options for personal

therapy or counselling. Friday, I will look into my own eat-sleep-exercise regime and decide what minor shift I can begin making.

5. Evaluate your current situation and determine a strategy to shift it. If boundaries, enabling behaviour, and/or codependency need attention, one strategy is to find yourself an advocate. You can work with them to develop a program for the shift. Just like the addict needs you as an advocate, you need your own support person to help you navigate this landscape. It could be a friend, a sibling, or a professional.

Wings

First, let's acknowledge that dealing with mental illnesses including addiction is very challenging. The worry sometimes turns into anxiety or depression and can be overwhelming. I hope my song inspires you to give yourself permission to be happy. Although the journeys are intertwined, we only get to control our own, and happiness is a choice (albeit sometimes a challenging one to make). Get the Kleenex box out.

WINGS

BY GAIL TAYLOR AND MALLORY BISHOP

I see you broken mother
and I've cried in the dark
A young son addicted
his life a question mark

And the father fighting demons
since his daughter was a teen
She's struggling in her thirties
His broken heart extreme

We saw beauty in their hearts
For glimpses they were gold
but the stronger we became
the more their use took hold

If only I could be his wings until he learned to fly
I wish I could be her wings to help her stay alive
But until they're ready to come back in
soar their own sky start again
then we have to be our wings
Our own wings

Years turned into decades
We very seldom spoke
and every time the phone rang
I hoped the spell had broke

We saw beauty in their hearts
For glimpses they were gold
but the stronger we became
the more their use took hold

If only I could be his wings until he learned to fly
I wish I could be her wings to help her stay alive
But until they're ready to come back in
soar their own sky start again
then we have to be our wings
Our own wings

Some of us are lucky
and our loved ones learned to fly
Some may not have made it and it's okay to cry
Some are out there using
while we're keeping hope alive
No matter the outcome our future's not defined

And our wings there still divine
we deserve to fly
To grant ourselves permission for soaring way up high
We will remember we may grieve
while we grant ourselves reprieve
Together we can be our wings
Yeah we can only be our wings

CHAPTER ELEVEN

Home Away from Home

What's in It for You—EVERYTHING

I'm opening up about my journey in giving back, hoping that my experiences can touch even one reader's heart and inspire their future choices.

Kindness can positively change your brain by boosting levels of serotonin and dopamine. These neurotransmitters produce feelings of satisfaction and well-being and cause the pleasure and reward centres in your brain to light up. Endorphins, your body's natural painkillers, also may be released when you show kindness. These combine to create something psychologists call "helper's high," and the rest of us recognize as the joy of giving.

My Story

In February of 2013, I first joined Rotary, an international organization that I found truly remarkable. After a few years of active involvement, I briefly stepped away, only to rediscover my passion for Rotary in the fall of 2023. Rotary's motto, "Service above self," serves as a constant reminder for me to prioritize helping others over personal interests. I adapted my own version of this with a mantra: "Service as part of self." This philosophy guided both my personal and professional life, and allowed me to participate in both my local and our global community.

I urge you to discover your own passion for giving back—a niche that nourishes your soul. Often, individuals who have experienced adversity firsthand are driven to support causes related to their own struggles. For me, this has manifested in a deep commitment in many areas, including mental health and addiction advocacy.

My personal journey illustrates how integrating service into one's life can be a natural and fulfilling endeavour. Throughout my career, I've had the privilege of serving on the boards of several non-profit organizations. My expertise in financial matters and fundraising enabled me to contribute in these areas. Discovering what to integrate into your life can often stem from unexpected sources.

A few years before my fiftieth birthday, I found myself feeling out of shape, prompting a decision to pursue physical fitness with renewed vigour. Setting my sights on running a marathon seemed like a fitting challenge. Despite having been inactive for some time, I resolved to embark on this ambitious endeavour. As I researched potential marathons, the TCS New York City Marathon stood out as the perfect opportunity. As I delved into my training regimen, I realized this was an opportunity to make a positive impact through fundraising. It dawned on me that I could use my marathon journey as a platform to support those in need. During my research, I stumbled upon an organization in Mexico that founded a program called "Children of the Dump," and, without hesitation, I dedicated myself to championing their cause.

This community in Puerto Vallarta, comprised of approximately 250 individuals, resided in close proximity to a landfill, where their daily routine involved scouring through the refuse for food and items to sell. The nonprofit organization I discovered was making a tangible difference in their lives by providing essential aid and educational opportunities. Their initiative began with offering daily food to the children, on the condition that they attend school and remain there throughout the day.

Inspired by their work, I resolved to combine my personal goal of achieving physical fitness with a fundraising goal to aid our neighbours to the south. Through the generosity of my network, I successfully raised $20,000 to support their cause. My husband, Harold, rightly pointed out that I should learn more about the organization, given the significant sum involved.

Taking his advice to heart, I decided to immerse myself in their community by embarking on a missionary trip. Arriving in Puerto Vallarta, I was initially overwhelmed by the dire conditions I encountered at the dump site. Witnessing preschool children playing amidst the garbage, surrounded by vultures flying above, evoked an emotional and physical reaction within me. Crying while trying not to vomit was the order of the day.

Despite my initial shock and discomfort, I persevered, determined to make a meaningful impact. Our days began at dawn, and we distributed food to those in need until late into the night. It was an intense and eye-opening experience, one that tested my resolve and pushed me beyond my comfort zone.

Reflecting on my journey, I realized the profound significance of stepping outside one's familiar surroundings and immersing oneself in the realities of others. It was a humbling experience that fuelled my determination to complete the New York City Marathon, knowing that every step I took would contribute to a cause greater than me.

Another amazing project for which I had the privilege of fundraising was an impactful initiative spearheaded by HealthBridge Foundation of Canada, an organization committed to combatting health disparities around the globe. Our focus was on Pakur, India, a region plagued by staggering rates of maternal, newborn, and child mortality—among the highest in the world. The heartbreaking reality is that many of these losses were preventable with simple, cost-effective health-care solutions. Yet, countless women and children remained tragically out of reach of these life-saving interventions.

The HealthBridge team worked tirelessly alongside local partners to bridge this gap, aiming to fortify the rural health-care infrastructure and foster a culture of proactive care-seeking. But it wasn't just about medical solutions; it was about empowering entire communities to prioritize the health and well-being of their loved ones. They endeavoured to mobilize not just women but also men and mothers-in-law, rallying them as allies in the fight for healthier futures.

The enormity of this mission weighed heavily on my heart as I became aware of not just the stark realities faced by families in this part of the world, but the amazing HealthBridge advocates on the other side of the globe stepping up to lend a hand. To me, that is nothing short of miraculous.

Tools for Thought

One of the most rewarding paths to personal growth is through giving back to others. Helping those less fortunate not only positively impacts their lives but also enriches yours. Engaging in acts of kindness and charity fosters a sense of gratitude, compassion, and connectedness.

Giving back doesn't always require grand gestures; small acts of kindness and support can have a profound impact on someone's life. As you help others, you'll find a sense of purpose and fulfillment that comes from making a positive difference in the world. Giving back is a two-way street that creates a sense of abundance and joy that propels you toward becoming your best self. Consider volunteering for causes close to your heart or supporting charitable organizations that align with your values.

There are so many people on this planet in need of help. Add to this our battered environment and animals that require care and protection, and there is no end to the volunteer possibilities. Hospitals, homeless shelters, places of worship, animal shelters, and local cleanup operations change our planet for the better.

If you simply want to volunteer and are not sure where to start the search, you might visit VolunteerMatch.org. A great feature of this site is its inclusion of both in-person and virtual volunteer opportunities. A virtual volunteer? People everywhere are talking to each other, face to face (via computer), teaching and learning a multitude of subjects. If you have a phone and an internet connection, you could help someone in another part of the world practise their conversational English skills for a few hours each week. It costs nothing to volunteer your time, but both parties benefit significantly from these interactions.

Share Your Talent

Fortunately, for all the types of help needed, there is someone with a knack for providing it. Every person has a talent. Some people are great at organizing information; others have the gift of the gab and can turn strangers into friends in minutes.

Any skills you have will benefit someone in need of them. We sometimes minimize our talents, even take them for granted. This is unfortunate, because one person's skill can become a gift to another person. When we view our abilities as contributions that others value, we feel joy that we have and can share them.

Do you play a musical instrument or a sport with a reasonable degree of proficiency? Do you speak more than one language (and do not forget sign language)? Organizations are looking for volunteers to share these skills and teach them to people who are eager to learn.

There is a saying about helping people help themselves and it is a truth worth remembering: feed someone a fish and you feed that person for a day, teach a person to fish and you feed that person for a lifetime. When we share our skills, we empower people. It is a shift in a positive direction, allowing us to move forward into a future with unlimited possibilities.

Financial Philanthropy

To be blunt, money is often an ideal problem-solver. It can make things work faster and better, it can make life easier and more comfortable. Money, like other tools, is neutral. People use hammers to pound nails into the beams that form the roofs of houses that shelter our families. They use money to buy the hammers and nails and roof shingles.

Donating time or a financial gift is equally beneficial in many cases. However, there are times when an organization's needs are urgent or unforeseen, and money may become the best answer.

Building Goodwill for Your Company

I never understood the concept that giving was better if it was anonymous. It is OK to be proud of your good deeds, as long as you do it in silence. As a fundraiser for many years, it made no difference to me if the funds came from altruistic motives or a quest for business or personal accolades.

A business could take out advertising in the local newspaper, or run radio spots or TV commercials to create awareness of their brand. Alternatively, they could sponsor a gala dinner for the local hospital or mental health project and have the corporation's name exposed in the event's marketing material, at the event, and in the annual report. The level of awareness may be the same, but now, the marketing dollars are doing good. How can that be wrong? I believe if you give back, help the world become just a little bit stronger, then we are all moving forward.

In my experience, watching entities step up, whether as a company or as individuals, inspires others to do the same. This is a good thing.

I do understand the benefits to anonymous charity, such as humility and the focus on the act itself rather than personal recognition; however, whether charity should be anonymous is subjective and depends on various factors, including cultural norms, personal beliefs, and the specific context of the charitable act.

Valid reasons why some people choose not to give anonymously include:

Accountability and Transparency: Non-anonymous giving allows donors to take credit for their contributions, which can help inspire trust and confidence in charitable organizations. Public acknowledgment of donations can also encourage others to support similar causes.

Inspiring Others: Visible acts of generosity can serve as powerful examples and inspire others to give. When individuals publicly share their charitable endeavours, it can create a ripple effect, mobilizing more people to get involved and make a difference.

Building Relationships: Openly supporting charitable causes can help individuals build meaningful connections with like-minded individuals and organizations. By sharing their philanthropic activities, donors may discover new opportunities for collaboration and collective impact.

Ultimately, whether your charitable endeavours are anonymous depends on your personal values, preferences, and the specific circumstances surrounding the act of giving. Both anonymous and non-anonymous forms of charity have their merits and can contribute to positive social change in different ways.

A good part of this book is about ideas, emotions, and specific areas of your life. On the other hand, giving and giving back are simply enormous and deeply rewarding. As appropriate as your boundaries can be, we are all still sharing a planet. Your life touches the lives of countless others. Giving back is more than a tool, it's a gamechanger. It is what moves humanity forward. I HOPE YOU WERE INSPIRED TO INSPIRE OTHERS WITH YOUR GIVING!

Home away from Home

The world is not equal, and the world is not fair. Many folks around the globe struggle for food, for water, for education, and in many other areas that you might take for granted. This song is acknowledging and respecting the local culture and people when you leave your neighbourhood.

HOME AWAY FROM HOME

BY GAIL TAYLOR AND MALLORY BISHOP

You know we view the world
through our own special lens
the five-star resorts can shine like precious gems
through the eyes of a tourist the beauty never ends
Adventures designed by those who know the trends

But the world is not that simple
some neighbors are in hell
So why not open up our hearts
and try to treat them well

The locals have the magic
full of charm and mystery
To ignore it would be tragic
let's learn their history
'Cause the world is our heaven
and wherever we roam
each location is a home away from home

We love to travel see the globe in its glory
German wineries and Ireland with pubs
Argentina's culture, man it tells a story
Islands where the penguins join the cool kids' club

Tokyo's fashion and skyline in Shanghai
The Taj Mahal, the pyramids and temples to explore
The whole Mediterranean opens up our eyes
Every new adventure leaves us wanting more

But the world is not that simple
some neighbors are in hell
So why not open up our hearts
and try to treat them well

The locals have the magic
full of charm and mystery
To ignore it would be tragic
let's learn their history
'Cause the world is our heaven
and wherever we roam
each location is a home away from home

Our home in North America
with coasts and open spaces
The majesty of mountains and cities full of flair
As we try to live our dreams
of course we think it's aces
But when we leave our neighborhood
let's show the world we care

The locals have the magic
full of charm and mystery
To ignore it would be tragic
let's learn their history
'Cause the world is our heaven
and wherever we roam
each location is a home away from home
Home away from home
A home away from home

SUMMARY - CHOICES

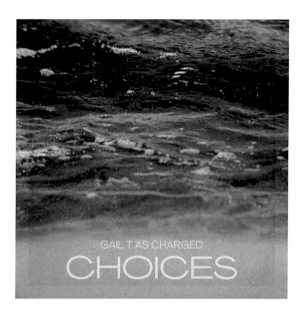

My Story

You and I both have several roles in our lives and each one can be defined differently, perhaps as a spouse, a partner, a parent, a grandparent, a sibling, a daughter or son, a friend, a colleague, or a neighbour. It is also your role to take care of your own emotional and physical well-being. Making that a priority makes you better with all your relationships. It elevates your compassion, your understanding, your energy, and your overall participation.

If I can inspire you to spend time designing the life you want, I'm living my passion and purpose. What's yours? Roles, responsibilities, work, self-care, play, call it what you want. IT'S LIFE! And the message I'm hitting you over the head with is, SHOW UP!

Show up and be accountable! When I realized that my happiness was my responsibility, not the job of people closest to me, it shifted something inside. I became less dependent on others for my happiness and became much happier, as did the people around me. It's amazing what life is like when you don't allow others to shift your mood. If someone cuts me off while driving, I look at the sky and say, "Universe, you owe me one," and smile genuinely. You don't control others' reactions, so why let them control yours?

One of the final stories I'll share was learning the true meaning of accountability. This can be a challenging lesson to embrace. I know it took me a while. In the mid-'90s I engaged in a multiday program called "Pursuit of Excellence," followed by "The Wall." One evening they had us participate in an exercise that involved taking our most challenging relationship, and developing a plan to move it forward in a healthy way that would allow us to feel empowered versus defeated. I chose to work on the then-dysfunctional relationship I had with my son Corey, who was still in active addiction. The exercise was structured in a way whereby all of the participants found a spot in the room to be alone and to work in silence. Once we had established our viable plan, we could go home.

This event started mid-day and, after working through the exercises, we were to bring our work to a facilitator and discuss the viability. I wasn't getting it. I tried several attempts to go home as I was exhausted, and thought my plan was great. She would ask me a few questions and send me back to my corner (literally) to figure it out. As I watched many of the other participants leave, starting around 5 p.m., I kept working on my plan. The goal was to develop a strategy on how I could decrease the confrontation, volatility, and emotional turmoil I was experiencing in communicating with Corey. I kept designing new options that all basically had the same theme: if I do this then, the result will be . . . because he will do . . .

Some of you already had the lightbulb go on when you read the above sentence and you know why I didn't get to go home until midnight. After several hours and a lot of tears, I figured it out. I didn't get to decide how my son was going to react to my actions any more than you get to decide how the people in your life will react to yours. That's out of our control, so designing our life means doing what works for us and accepting the consequences of others' reactions. The program that taught me that lesson was designed to force me to figure it out myself and that was a gamechanger. From that point on I went through life aware that my life, and my reactions, all of them, were on me.

We ended that program with a kumbaya moment of harmony and unity. The final session involved an emotional exercise whereby I was on the floor lying on my back and was lifted off the ground by my colleagues, and then rocked back and forth while they blasted Carole King's song "Child of Mine" throughout the room.

I shared a lot of my life's journey in this book, and I know that many of you have your own version of a similar story. You make choices every day, some big and some small, some that work out and some that just become lessons learned. Designing your best life is an option that might require some shifts in the choices you make going forward and I challenge you to take that step. It's amazing how fun it can be.

There is a "thinking" option that suggests you can shift from *either/ or to both/and,* allowing you to move past choosing option one or option two and, rather, embracing both. It's a theory that you can take care of a struggling loved one (maybe with Alzheimer's) while maintaining your own daily happiness and the fun in your life. Another is working through serious health issues and planning your next adventure.

When I made the choice to come out of retirement at the age of sixty-four, I kept hearing about ageism and how anyone over forty had limited opportunities in the world. I decided to do what I always did and ask the question, "How can I turn this into an opportunity?" It worked. Here is the headline of a press release that resulted in media and podcast interviews.

New Song - Writer Gail Taylor at Sixty Five is Releasing Her Third Country Music Single "Staying Young" - October 1st, 2021

September 22, 2021 12:17 ET | Source: Gail Taylor Music

Edmonton, Alberta, September 22nd, 2021 (Globenewswire): **Gail Taylor,** a Canadian entrepreneur, philanthropist and song-writer is excited to announce the third release of her Five-Single Country Music Series. The inspirational, "feel-good" tune is called "Staying Young" and reflects the attitude she used to reinvent herself as a musician at an age when others are winding down.

The song was written to inspire others to smile and enjoy the moment and most importantly, follow your dreams no matter what stage you are at in life. Gail, at age 65 lives by her own lyrics as she moves confidently into her new calling in the music industry after a lifelong career in finance. The new musician **began sharing her outgoing personality and song writing talents with the world** under the stage name *"Gail T as Charged."*

Allow me a final share and a glimpse of my musical journey, beginning with an invitation from my husband, Harold, to accompany him to a cochlear implants conference in Nashville back in the spring of 2019. Given my passion for music and desire to enhance my songwriting skills, I embarked on a quest to find guidance while in Nashville. After diligent research, I connected with Mallory Tunnell, a talented singer/songwriter and teacher willing to dedicate three days to working with me. Little did I know Mallory would become not only a lifelong mentor but also a dear friend and cowriter, contributing her vocals to several tracks, including the titular song of this chapter, "Choices."

Following months of collaboration with Mallory via Zoom, I felt compelled to breathe life into my compositions. Thus, I sought the expertise of Beaird Music Studios in Nashville. Embracing an unconventional approach, I navigated the recording process despite lacking traditional musical skills. To distinguish my project from the norm, I adopted the moniker, "Gail T as Charged," a playful nod to the unconventional nature of my endeavour.

With the aid of modern technology, I independently distributed my music across various streaming platforms, even before I had enough talent to play in the compositions. Collaborating with seasoned musicians from Beaird Music Studio, whose credentials included associations with industry luminaries such as Tim McGraw and Miranda Lambert, felt like a dream come true.

Additionally, the graciousness of Alberta's local celebrity Danny Hooper, who readily agreed to lend his vocals to one of my early compositions, left an indelible mark on my journey. While some milestones, like the song Danny sang, "Love for Country Music," remain outside the confines of this narrative, each experience has shaped my artistic evolution.

Another dream come true was a fruitful songwriting collaboration with Carolyn Dawn Johnson, a Canadian country singer/songwriter icon. We wrote this final chapter's song "Choices," a testament to the serendipitous connections forged along the way, together.

Over the past five years, Nashville has become a part of my journey in music. It's a place where I've honed my craft—both in Mallory's music studio on Music Row and Beaird Music Studio down the road. I also transformed my basement into a personal music studio, where I spend hours each day in pursuit of creativity, be it writing new songs, refining my piano skills, or fine-tuning my public-speaking abilities.

In sharing my journey, I hope I have inspired you to embrace your own creative paths, navigating the highs and lows with resilience and an unwavering commitment to crafting a life filled with magic and purpose.

Choices

This song was written shortly after COVID, AKA "one of the sharks," when many people were forced to reinvent themselves overnight. TALK ABOUT A CURVEBALL! Knowing how to embrace every chapter and change in your life and make the choices that will create your best life is the superpower. It's not the curveballs that matter – it's what you do with them.

CHOICES

BY GAIL TAYLOR AND CAROLYN DAWN JOHNSON

Waking up, wondering where the day will go
In my head thoughts that helped me stay afloat
Can I, can I, can I rise above the noise that's deafening?
I know, I know, I know the world is spinning like a storm at sea

Do I have to take it in to feel like I belong
or can I somehow stay aware without consuming all the wrong?

All the choices I have to make to keep my head above the water
while all the sharks are underneath and they're trying to pull me under, under
If we could back things up, a different world would be
maybe we could change the trajectory
That ain't the way it works, forward it will be
if anything's going to change, it's up to you and me

Looking around seems that others have found bliss
Are they for real? How can they still dance and sing and kiss?
I have my own big dreams that I would like to see come true
What's the secret formula for blowing past the blues?

All the choices I have to make to keep my head above the water
while all the sharks are underneath and they're trying to pull me under, under
If we could back things up, a different world would be
maybe we could change the trajectory
That ain't the way it works, forward it will be
If anything's going to change, it's up to you and me

All the choices I have to make to keep my head above the water
while all the sharks are underneath and they're trying to pull me under, under
If we could back things up, a different world would be
maybe we could change the trajectory
That ain't the way it works, forward it will be
If anything's going to change, it's up to you and me
Oh if it's gonna change, it's up to you and me
If it's going to change, it's up to you and me

ACKNOWLEDGEMENTS

Throughout the process of writing this book I've joked about "not knowing writing a book would take so much time." It was an amazing undertaking, and I couldn't have done it alone. I was so fortunate to have an amazing network to help me through the process.

I am so grateful to my friend and life coach, Vicki Schmitt, who wrote the foreword. We had weekly Zoom calls where we bounced around different sections, and her amazing insights helped me articulate my ideas at a higher level.

I would like to thank Suzanne Busch, a writer, an editor, and a wonderful contributor who helped me create a finished product I can be proud of.

When I started down the journey of creating this book, it was suggested to me that I have as many eyes as possible review sections throughout the writing process. This resulted in many positive edits and many improvements to the content and for this I thank Paula Bourgeault, Joanne Bourgeault, Laura Brown, Corey Henwood, Harold Taylor, and Deanna Clee.

. . . and to my Nashville friends: I thank Mallory Trunnell, songwriter, producer, instructor, amazing vocalist, and musician for sharing in my music journey and being such an integral part of my songs as a cowriter, sometimes vocalist, and always there to help me level up. I thank Lauren Harding of Dance Magick Media for creating the exceptional images and videos for each and every song.

Lastly, I thank Samuel Beck, for working with me from day one and helping me keep every thing moving forward.

Thank you to all the Kickstarter supporters that helped make this book possible. Having you in my corner means so much. You're all AWESOME!

Arlene and Doreen Breitkreuz
Brandon St-Louis
Brian Boucher
Bruce Bourgeault
Celine Ruest and James Brittle
Cheryl Raiwet
Claire and Richard Murphy
Corey and Julie Henwood
Danny Hooper
Deanna Clee
Denis Regimbal
Donna Bourgeault and Rene Miron
Donna Gehmlich
Dorothy and Ron Kubsch
Fred Patton
Georgina Johnston
Harold Taylor
Jake Miron
Janice Ricken and Martin Wood
Joanne Bourgeault
Judy Bain
Judy Smallwood
Kathy Strobl
Khanh Tran
Laura Brown and Guillaume Couture
Lynn Bourgeault
Mallory Trunnell
Paula Bourgeault
Samuel and Victoria Beck
Sarah Bonhet
Sean Bourgeault
Shantell Bourgeault and Connor Warwick
Sharen and Gary Machney
Simon Atuhairwe
Sky McLaughlin
Sylvia St Martin
Thelma Bourgeault
Vicki and Chris Schmitt

BIBLIOGRAPHY/
RECOMMENDED READING

I didn't invent any of the life-changing ideas that I implemented into my life, and shared with you throughout this book. Below, although not exhaustive, is a list of material that helped shape my journey to living my best life.

PERSONAL GROWTH AND PEAK PERFORMANCE

Blanchard, Ken. *Zap the Gaps! Target Higher Performance and Achieve It!* (2002). William Morrow. ISBN 978-0060503000.

Carnegie, Dale. *How to Win Friends and Influence People* (1936). Simon & Schuster. ISBN 1-4391-6734-6.

Chopra, Deepak. *The Seven Spiritual Laws of Success* (1994). New World Library. ISBN 978-1878424112.

Clason, George. The Richest Man in Babylon (1926). Penguin Books. ISBN 978-0451205360

Covey, Stephen, Merrill, Roger A., Merrill, Rebecca R. *First Things First* (1994). Free Press. ISBN 0-684-80203-1.

Covey, Stephen. *Seven Habits of Highly Effective People* (1989). Free Press. ISBN 0-7432-6951-9.

Dyer, Wayne. *Wishes Fulfilled; Mastering the Art of Manifesting* (2012). Hay House LLC. ISBN 978-1401937287.

Hendricks, Gay. *The Big Leap* (2010). HarperOne. ISBN 978-0061735363.

Hill, Napoleon. *Think and Grow Rich* (1937). The Ralston Society. ISBN 978-1-78844-102-5.

Kotler, Steven. *The Art of Impossible* (2021). Harper. ISBN 978-0062977533.

Manson, Mark. *The Subtle Art of Not Giving a F*ck: A Counterintuitive Approach to Living a Good Life* (2016). Harper. ISBN 978-0062457714.

Nightingale, Earl. *The Essence of Success: 163 Life Lessons from the Dean of Self-Development* (1993). Nightingale-Conant Corp. ISBN 9781555254568.

Olinekova, Gayle. *Go For It!* (1982). Simon & Schuster. ISBN 0-671-45692-X.

Peale, Norman Vincent. *The Power of Positive Thinking* (2023). Touchstone. ISBN 978-0743234801.

Robbins, Tony. *Awaken the Giant Within: How to Take Immediate Control of Your Mental, Emotional, Physical and Financial Destiny!* (1992). Simon & Schuster. ISBN 978-0671791544.

Robbins, Tony. *Unlimited Power* (1997). Free Press. ISBN 978-0684845777.

Rohn, Jim. *7 Strategies For Wealth and Happiness* (1996). Brolga Publishing. ISBN 9781921221118.

Ruiz, Miguel Don. *The Four Agreements: A Practical Guide to Personal Freedom* (1997). Amber-Allen Publishing. ISBN 9781878424310.

Tolle, Eckhart. *The Power of Now: A Guide to Spiritual Enlightenment* (2004). New World Library. ISBN 978-1577314806.

Tracy, Brian. Goals!: *How to Get Everything You Want—Faster Than You Ever Thought Possible* (2010). Berrett-Koehler Publishers. ISBN 978-1605094113.

Ziglar, Zig. *Goals: How to Get the Most Out of Your Life* (2020). Sound Wisdom. ISBN 978-1640951266.

MENTAL HEALTH AND ADDICTION

Trimpey, Jack. *Rational Recovery: The New Cure for Substance Addiction* (1996). Gallery Books. ISBN 978-0671528584.

Maisel, Eric and Raeburn, Susan. *Creative Recovery: A Complete Addiction Treatment Program That Uses Your Natural Creativity* (2008). Trumpeter. ISBN 978-1590305447.

Larson Matthews, Joan. *Seven Weeks to Sobriety: The Proven Program to Fight Alcoholism through Nutrition* (1997). Ballantine Books. ISBN 978-0449002599.

DuPont, Robert L., DuPont Spencer, Elizabeth, M.D. DuPont, Caroline, M. *The Anxiety Cure: An Eight-Step Program for Getting Well* (2003). John Wiley & Sons, Inc. ISBN 978-0471464877.

Kolk van der, Bessel. *The Body Keeps the Score: Brain, Mind and Body in the Healing of Trauma* (2014). Viking. ISBN 978-0670785933.

Hari, Johann. *Lost Connections: Uncovering the Real Causes of Depression—and the Unexpected Solutions* (2018). Bloomsbury USA. ISBN 978-1632868305.

NOTES

Introduction
Harvard Health
https://www.health.harvard.edu/blog/why-is-music-good-for-the-brain-2020100721062

Chapter 1 – The Game of Life
Billie Eilish, Lady Gaga, and David Bowie – imposter syndrome
https://commons.bcit.ca/evolution1079/2023/11/14/imposter-syndrome-musicians-biggest-enemy/#:~:text=Even%20Grammy%20Awards%20winners%20like,tend%20to%20think%20the%20worst
Anna Mary Robertson Moses
https://nmwa.org/art/artists/grandma-moses-anna-mary-robertson-moses/#:~:text=She%20gained%20the%20nickname%20"Grandma,her%20death%20at%20age%20101
Clint Eastwood
https://www.remindmagazine.com/article/4454/clint-eastwood-last-film-juror-2/
Betty White
https://www.newretirement.com/retirement/advice-from-betty-white-on-not-retiring-aging-well-and-living-a-happy-life/#:~:text=While%20she%20was%20associated%20with,school%20through%20her%20final%20year
Mick Jagger
https://www.theguardian.com/music/2023/oct/20/the-more-children-you-have-the-more-laissez-faire-you-get-mick-jagger-on-ageing-rage-and-missing-charlie-watts

Chapter 2: Dreamin' Bout the Good Life
Bronnie Ware
https://bronnieware.com/blog/regrets-of-the-dying/
Adult Regrets
https://www.deseret.com/2014/7/20/20544945/seniors-are-in-search-of-a-re-do-survey-finds-older-americans-wish-they-could-change-some-things/

New Year's Eve resolution
https://www.gq-magazine.co.uk/lifestyle/article/new-years-resolution-habit-linking
Covey, Stephen R., Merrill, Roger A., Merrill, Rebecca R. *First Things First*. Free Press. ISBN 0684802031.

Chapter 3: Flipped Upside Right
GET strategy Goals, Emotions, To-Do List. Inspired by Tony Robbins RPM and
Napoleon Hill
https://www.naphill.org/shop/books/paperback/napoleon-hills-guide-to-achieving-your-goals-live-a-life-that-matters-book-2/
Tony Robbins - RPM
https://www.tonyrobbins.com/pdfs/Workbook-Time-of-your-Life.pdf
Myers-Briggs
https://www.themyersbriggs.com/en-US/Products-and-Services/Myers-Briggs

Chapter 4: Let Your Freak Flag Fly
Rohn, Jim
7 Strategies For Wealth and Happiness. Brolga Publishing. ISBN 9781921221118
John Donne
https://allpoetry.com/No-man-is-an-island

Chapter 5: Ambition's Not A Four-Letter Word
MIT study - credit card spending
https://mitsloan.mit.edu/experts/how-credit-cards-activate-reward-center-our-brains-and-drive-spending
Nortel
https://en.wikipedia.org/wiki/Nortel
Bre-X
https://en.wikipedia.org/wiki/Bre-X

Chapter 6: You and You Alone
Dale Carnegie
https://www.dalecarnegie.com

Chapter 7: Staying Young

Margot Kidder
https://en.wikipedia.org/wiki/Margot_Kidder
Brain cell function
https://medicine.wustl.edu/news/neurons-help-flush-waste-out-of-brain-during-sleep/#:~:text=There%20lies%20a%20paradox%20in,of%20heightened%20brain%20cell%20function

Problem-solving while we sleep citation link
https://www.sciencedaily.com/releases/2011/06/110607094849.htm
Sleep and memory citation link
https://www.ncbi.nlm.nih.gov/pmc/articles/PMC311359/#:~:text=Because%20late%20sleep%20is%20dominated,emotional%20memories%20(Grieser%20et%20al
Exercise and antidepressants
https://www.health.harvard.edu/mind-and-mood/exercise-is-an-all-natural-treatment-to-fight-depression
Junk food may worsen depression
https://www.hopementalhealth.com/blog/junk-food-might-be-causing-your-anxiety-and-depression

Chapter 8: Time Is on My Side
Stephen Covey's – four Quadrants
https://www.franklincovey.com/the-7-habits/habit-3/
underestimating task time
https://zapier.com/blog/how-to-estimate-time/

Chapter 9: You're My Best Investment
General George S. Patton
https://quotefancy.com/quote/815559/George-S-Patton-Jr-Say-what-you-mean-and-mean-what-you-say

Chapter 10: Wings
Psychology Today definition of codependency
https://www.psychologytoday.com/us/basics/codependency#:~:text=Codependent%20relationships%2C%20on%20the%20other,one's%20irresponsible%20or%20destructive%20behavior.

Naloxone
https://www.camh.ca/en/health-info/mental-illness-and-addiction-index/naloxone
Johann Hari
https://johannhari.com

Summary: Choices
Either/or versus both/and
https://www.psychologytoday.com/ca/blog/between-the-generations/202102/what-is-bothand-thinking
Pursuit of Excellence and The Wall
https://www.contextinternational.com/i-the-pursuit-of-excellence.html

INDEX

ABOUT THE AUTHOR

Gail Taylor is a Canadian songwriter, keynote speaker, entrepreneur, and author celebrated for her vibrant personality and musical creations that inspire others to take charge of their personal and professional lives. With forty years of studying the art of personal growth and peak performance, she is living proof that designing your own life is within reach, no matter your beginnings.

In her early sixties, Gail chose to reinvent herself, embarking on new journeys in music, public speaking, and writing. Driven by a passion for helping others, she shares stories and tools designed to inspire people to reach their next level. Gail's techniques have enabled her to avoid stress and burnout, fostering a positive lifestyle. She openly shares personal stories about overcoming challenges, including self-destructive behaviors and family addiction. Gail believes in the importance of making mistakes on the path to success and emphasizes inner growth and acceptance.

Before transitioning to the creative world of writing and speaking, Gail was a vice president and financial advisor at CIBC Wood Gundy for 25 years. She built a successful investment advisory practice within their corporate structure, managing investment portfolios for high-net-worth individuals.

Gail has spent decades dedicated to personal development and education. She earned a Certified Investment Manager Analyst (CIMA) designation from Wharton University, an MBA from Queen's University, completed executive training in micro-finance at Harvard Business School, and more recently has completed several programs at Berklee's online music school.

Her extensive experience in personal betterment, goal-setting, and living with passion and purpose has made her a sought-after guest on numerous podcasts. Gail has just completed her second book and continues to inspire others with her journey and insights.